MARX for beginners

Writers and Readers Publishing Co operative

this translation published by:
WRITERS AND READERS PUBLISHING CO OPERATIVE (SOCIETY LIMITED)

English translation by:
RICHARD APPIGNANESI; Copyright © 1976

transcription and design by:
The Hackney Trucking Company, 25 Wayland Avenue, London E8

typesetting by:
JETSET, 38 KING STREET, LONDON WC2

printed by:
COX AND WYMAN LTD, NORWICH ROAD, FAKENHAM, NORFOLK

WE WISH TO THANK NICK JACOBS FOR HIS UNFAILING HELP

WRITERS AND READERS PUBLISHING COOPERATIVE, (SOCIETY LIMITED),
14 TALACRE ROAD, LONDON NW5 3PE, ENGLAND

PREFACE...

WHAT?! TRY TO SUMMARIZE MARX? THAT'S NOT ONLY A SACRILEGE (AS MOST "ACADEMIC" MARXISTS WILL SAY), BUT A COMPLETE WASTE OF TIME — BECAUSE COMRADE KARL IS SUPPOSED TO BE COMPLETELY BEYOND THE RANGE OF SIMPLE MINDS.

MAYBE SO, MAYBE NOT. BUT I'VE WRITTEN THIS BOOK ANYWAY, ON THE PRINCIPLE THAT THE WORST KIND OF BATTLE IS THE ONE NOT CONFRONTED.

ANOTHER REASON FOR TRYING TO TAKE ON CHARLIE WAS MY WISH TO UNDERSTAND HIM — AN AMBITION WHICH I HAVEN'T SATISFIED.

MARX — LADIES AND GENTS — WAS TRULY A "TOUGH GUY". A "TEUTONIC GENIUS" TOWERING OVER MUCH OF THE SCIENTIFIC KNOWLEDGE OF HIS DAY. HE JUST WENT ON PRODUCING PHILOSOPHY ON PHILOSOPHY, WITHOUT WORRYING HOW MANY PEOPLE WOULD UNDERSTAND HIM. RESULT? A WHOLE SERIES OF HIGH-LEVEL WORKS. REALLY HEAVY STUFF AND MUCH TOO DENSE FOR THE ORDINARY READER. MARX IS HARD TO DIGEST!

THIS BOOK TRIES TO PROVIDE A "DIGEST" — AN EXTRACT OF MARX'S IDEAS. SOMETHING EASIER TO GET DOWN. BEING AWARE OF MY LIMITS (5th. GRADE ELEMENTARY!), I AM HAPPY IF THE THING ISN'T COMPLETELY INCOMPREHENSIBLE.

MARX HIMSELF HASN'T MADE MY JOB ANY EASIER BY FORGETTING TO PROVIDE A SUMMARY OF HIS WORKS. I GOT EVEN LESS HELP FROM ALL THOSE SCHOLARLY VOLUMES WHICH PRETEND TO CLARIFY MARX, BUT END UP BEING MORE DIFFICULT THAN CHARLIE HIMSELF.

AN ATTEMPT TO "POPULARIZE" MARX RAISES ANOTHER PROBLEM — THE DIFFICULTY OF PUTTING INTO EVERYDAY LANGUAGE THE PHILOSOPHIC AND ECONOMIC TERMS HE USES. BECAUSE THERE AREN'T ONLY 20 OR 30, BUT 200 OR 300! TO TRY TRANSLATING THIS NUMBER WITHOUT LOSING THEIR MEANING IS REALLY DOG WORK. I HOPE THE AVERAGE READER WHO GETS THROUGH THIS BOOK WILL HAVE THE COURAGE TO CONFRONT THE COMPLETE WORKS OF MARX AND COME OUT OF IT BETTER THAN I DID.

I SHOULD ALSO LIKE TO THANK THE ILLUSTRIOUS MARXIST THEORETICIANS WHO, WHEN I ASKED THEM FOR A HAND, REPLIED POLITELY THAT I MUST BE OUT OF MY MIND TO START SUCH A WORK. I REALLY APPRECIATE THEIR "SPIRIT OF CO-OPERATION" AND REGRET NOT HEEDING THEIR ADVICE BEFORE SETTLING DOWN WITH HERR DOKTOR KARL MARX.

AFTER THIS INTRODUCTION, IF YOU STILL WANT TO GO ON READING— BE WARNED! YOU DO SO AT YOUR OWN RISK. I CANNOT ANSWER FOR THE DAMAGES.

ONE LAST EXCUSE FOR THIS LIGHT-WEIGHT BOOK (BESIDE MY OWN IGNORANCE): THE STUBBORN AND INSISTENT PRESSURE OF MY PUBLISHER WHO LEFT ME HARDLY ANY TIME TO WRITE IT. I'M SORRY TO SEE MY EFFORTS HAVEN'T "JELLED" AS I WOULD HAVE LIKED.

IT'S INCREDIBLE THAT MARX, WORKING UNDER FAR WORSE CONDITIONS AND PRESSURES THAN MINE, COULD WRITE ALL THOSE *THOUSANDS* OF PAGES WITHOUT EVER LOSING HIS WAY OR MAKING A BOTCH OF IT.

BUT THAT JUST GOES TO PROVE IN THE END THAT MARX IS MARX, A RIUS IS... WELL, JUST A POOR GUY!

FIRST THINGS FIRST—
THE READER WOULD
LIKE TO KNOW WHO
THIS
CHARACTER
MARX WAS!!
Wasn't he one
of the MARX
Brothers?

Karl Marx
Hmm... well... not exactly...

CHARLES MARX ('KARL' AS HE'S CALLED IN GERMAN) WAS A JEWISH-GERMAN PHILOSOPHER WHO LIVED AND STRUGGLED FROM 1818 TO 1883. EVERYWHERE IN THE WORLD HE'S BLAMED FOR HAVING INVENTED

COMMUNISM....

BASED ON HIS WRITINGS AND IDEAS, ONE THIRD OF HUMANITY PRACTISES COMMUNISM, WHILE THE OTHER TWO THIRDS KEEP ARGUING ABOUT THEM...

ANYWHERE YOU GO, WORDS LIKE BOLSHEVIK, MARXIST, SOCIALISM, LENINISM, RED, FIDELISTS, MAOIST, MATERIALIST, COMMUNIST AND SO ON RUB LOTS OF PEOPLE UP THE WRONG WAY...

ACTUALLY, MARXISM TODAY DIVIDES THE WORLD INTO TWO CAMPS: THOSE WHO HATE HIM AND THOSE WHO PLACE ALL THEIR HOPES IN HIM...
and I'd mention a third group: those who don't know him...
BECAUSE CHARLIE MARX IS JUST LIKE THE BIBLE OR THE KORAN: MANY QUOTE HIM, BUT VERY FEW KNOW HIM, AND EVEN FEWER UNDERSTAND HIM... (OR BETTER... MAKE HIM OUT...)
MARX HAS SOMETHING TO SAY TO EVERYBOD THERE'S NOT A MAJOR CHANGE IN THE LAST HUNDRED YEARS WHICH DOESN'T OWE SOMETHING TO COMRADE CHARLIE'S INFLUENCE...
ECONOMY, LITERATURE, SPACE TRAVEL, THE ARTS, HISTORY, HUMAN RELATIONS, THE VATICAN, THE UNIONS, REVOLUTIONS, SOCIAL CHANGES, EDUCATION, MEDICINE, INDUSTRY, AGRICULTURE, JOURNALISM... EVERYWHERE YOU'LL FIND A HAIR OR TWO OF CHARLIE'S!!
Boy! He sure had lots of interests, the hairy old guy!
And he wasn't short of hair...!

KNOWLEDGE – AND PRACTICE – OF HIS IDEAS NOW MAKES POSSIBLE WHAT WAS IMPOSSIBLE FOR TWENTY CENTURIES: FREEDOM FROM THE EXPLOITATION OF MAN BY MAN...

IN SHORT: IF IN EVERY SENSE WE'RE BETTER OFF TODAY, WE OWE THAT TO MARX ESPECIALLY...

(SOCIAL SECURITY, PENSIONS, PAID HOLIDAYS, UNIONS, SCHOLARSHIPS, AND MANY OTHER VICTORIES ARE INDIRECTLY DUE TO MARX!)

ALL REVOLUTIONS, EVEN THOSE WHICH CLAIM TO BE SPONTANEOUS AND WITHOUT "PUTATIVE" FATHERS, HAVE A MARXIST ORIGIN...

WORKER PRIESTS ARE ACCUSED OF BEING MARXISTS, SOUTH AMERICAN GENERALS TALK ABOUT HIM.
HE'S STUDIED IN JESUIT SCHOOLS.
OTHERS HAVE FLED CUBA WHEN IT DECLARED ITSELF THE FIRST MARXIST COUNTRY IN LATIN AMERICA...
BUT STILL YOU HEAR IT SAID THERE'S NO INTEREST IN MARX...

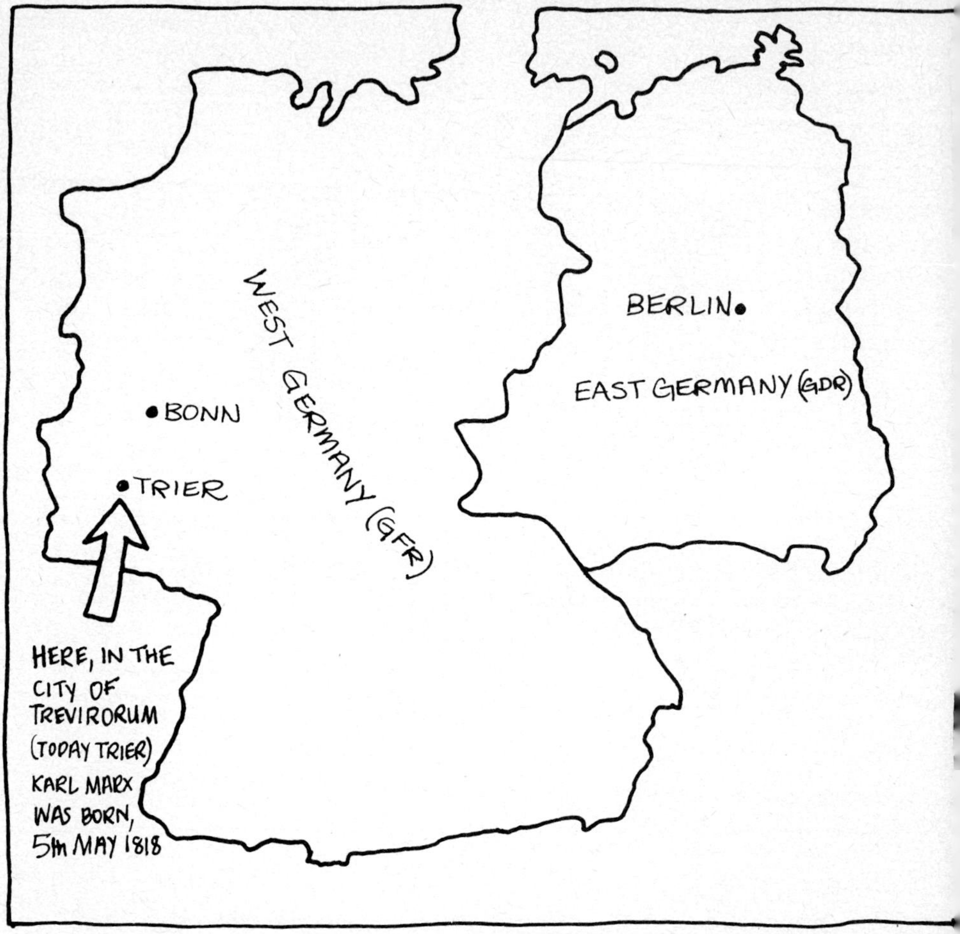

HIS FATHER WAS A WELL-TO-DO LAWYER, WHICH ALLOWED THE YOUNG MARX TO STUDY WHAT WAS IN FASHION THEN:

LAW.

FROM BONN HE WENT TO BERLIN WHERE HE FINISHED HIS STUDIES. THEN HE RETURNED TO BONN TO TRY TEACHING, BUT HIS BAD NAME DIDN'T OPEN ANY DOORS: IN BERLIN HE'D TURNED ATHEIST AND SUBVERSIVE...

THAT WAS TOO MUCH! HIS SOCIETY BARELY TOLERATED ARTISTS, SO JUST IMAGINE WHAT THEY MADE OF *SUBVERSIVES*!!!

IT IS IMPORTANT AT THIS POINT TO CLEAR UP A DETAIL ABOUT MARX'S LIFE: ALTHOUGH HIS ORIGINS WERE JEWISH, HE DIDN'T CONSIDER HIMSELF JEWISH, OR EVER PRACTISE THAT RELIGION. HIS FATHER HAD BECOME A LUTHERAN AND MARX HIMSELF WAS ONE, BUT ONLY IN HIS YOUTH...
How true! Youngsters today dont believe a damn thing!
Blame the idealogies, your lordship, the ideologies...

THE UNIVERSITY OF BERLIN WAS IN A TERRIFIC TURMOIL OF NEW IDEAS. RELIGIOUS EXPLANATIONS OF MAN AND THE UNIVERSE HAD BEEN CHALLENGED AND THINKERS WERE LOOKING ROUND FOR OTHER ANSWERS TO THE ETERNAL QUESTIONS OF MANKIND...
The same old eternal questions
Who is God?
Life is a Riddle
What is Man?
Why do we live?
What is Life?

TO ANSWER THIS THORNY QUESTION, MARX DECIDED TO STUDY PHILOSOPHY...

HIS FATHER GROWS ANGRY WORRYING ABOUT HIS SON'S FUTURE...

SOMEONE CALLED FREDERICK HEGEL SEEMS TO HAVE FOUND THE ANSWERS TO THE BIG QUESTIONS.
GERMAN PHILOSOPHERS GRAVITATE ROUND HIM, SOME TO OPPOSE AND OTHERS TO SUPPORT HIS THEORIES...
MARX BEGINS STUDYING HEGEL'S IDEAS.
TOO BAD THE GREAT PHILOSOPHER HAD ALREADY DIED, ALAS!...

COMING AFTER KANT, WHO HAD DENIED GOD'S EXISTENCE BECAUSE NO SYSTEM COULD *PROVE* IT, HEGEL INSTEAD SEEKS TO JUSTIFY GOD'S EXISTENCE PHILOSOPHICALLY...

(Note: at the end of this book the reader will find a little dictionary of philosophical terms, should any uncertainties arise)

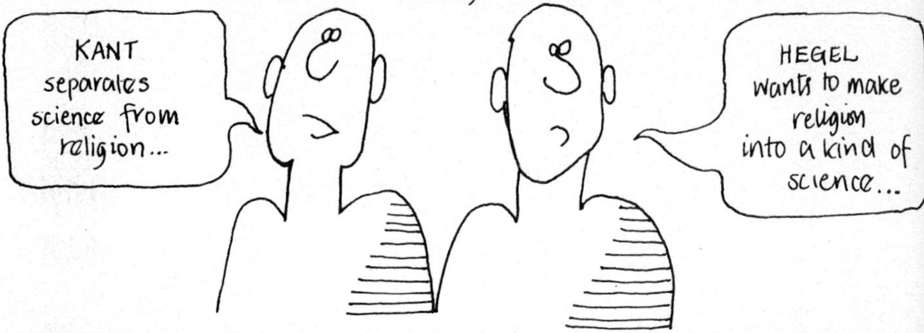

TO PUT IT ANOTHER WAY: HEGEL WANTED TO PROVE GOD'S EXISTENCE THROUGH PHILOSOPHY, BUT OUTSIDE RELIGION... HEGEL JUSTIFIES BELIEF IN A GOOD GOD, BUT HE FINDS NO JUSTIFICATION FOR RELIGION...

OF COURSE, ALL THE CHURCHES PROTEST AND RUSH TO CONDEMN HEGEL!

Marx's student friend Köppen (caricature by Engels)

HEGEL SAYS THAT GOD'S CONSCIOUSNESS OF GOD IS NONE OTHER THAN THE CONSCIOUSNESS MAN HAS OF GOD — IN OTHER WORDS — GOD BECAME CONSCIOUS OF HIS EXISTENCE *THROUGH* MAN...

BESIDES WHICH, HEGEL DIDN'T BELIEVE IN THE IMMORTALITY OF THE SOUL. BUT PERSECUTED BY THE CHURCH AND STATE (IN THOSE DAYS ALLIED), HE WAS FORCED TO GIVE IN A BIT AND NOT ALLOW HIS IDEAS TO BE SPREAD AMONG THE PEOPLE. HIS IDEAS WERE – SO HE SAID – "NOTHING MORE THAN PHILOSOPHY" AND IT WAS NECESSARY THAT PEOPLE SHOULD STILL FOLLOW THEIR CUSTOMARY RELIGION...

BUT IT WAS REALLY HEGEL'S PHILOSOPHY OF HISTORY WHICH ATTRACTED MARX. ACCORDING TO HEGEL, HUMANITY ADVANCES AND PROGRESSES ONLY BECAUSE OF CONFLICTS, WARS, REVOLUTIONS; THAT IS, THROUGH THE STRUGGLE OF THE OPPRESSED AGAINST OPPRESSORS.

PEACE AND HARMONY – HE USED TO SAY – DON'T MAKE FOR PROGRESS...

HEGEL WASN'T TALKING ABOUT SOCIAL STRUGGLE, BUT ONLY ABOUT *RELIGIOUS* STRUGGLE. HE WASN'T THINKING OF THE STRUGGLES BETWEEN WORKERS AND BOSSES, BETWEEN OPPRESSED PEOPLES AND OPPRESSIVE GOVERNMENTS... ONLY OF A PURELY "SPIRITUAL" CONFLICT, A STRUGGLE BETWEEN IDEAS...

WHEN HEGEL DIED, CONTRADICTIONS LIKE THESE DIVIDED HIS FOLLOWERS INTO "HEGELIANS OF THE RIGHT" AND "LEFT". THE LEFT DEFENDED THEIR TEACHER'S MOST PROGRESSIVE IDEAS, THE RIGHT STUCK TO HEGEL'S SPIRITUAL AND CONSERVATIVE SIDE...

LUDWIG FEUERBACH, A SUPPORTER OF THE HEGELIAN LEFT, WANTS TO PUT HEGEL'S THEORY INTO PRACTICE. HE DENIES THE "SACRED" ORIGIN OF ROYAL AUTHORITY.
MARX IS 100% WITH HIM...

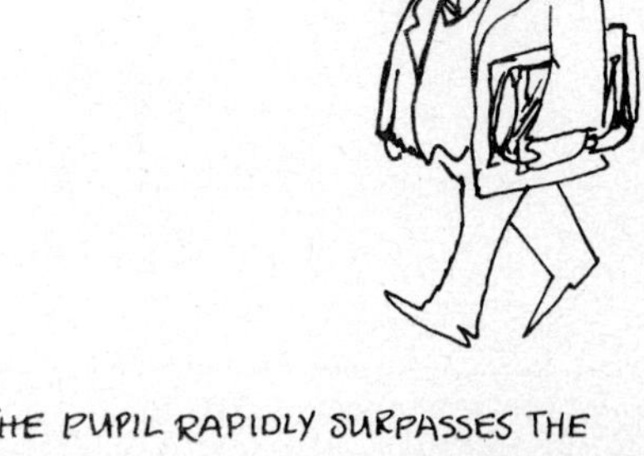

THE PUPIL RAPIDLY SURPASSES THE TEACHER: MARX IS MORE RADICAL, MORE CLEAR-HEADED AND MORE PRACTICAL THA THE HEGELIAN LEFTISTS. MARX IS THE ACTIVE TYPE AND NOT ONE FOR BLAH BLAH BLAH BLAH BLAH....

THE HEGELIANS GOT LOST IN ENDLESS PHILOSOPHICAL AND THEOLOGICAL DEBATES: THEIR MEETINGS ALWAYS FINISHED WITH MORE SMOKE THAN FIRE... TO AVOID ENDING UP NEUROTIC, MARX ACCEPTED A JOB ON THE "RHENISH GAZETTE"... THAT WAS IN 1842

MARX MADE SUCH AN IMPACT ON THE EDITORIAL COMMITTEE THAT HE WAS SOON MADE EDITOR-IN-CHIEF. UNDER HIS DIRECTION THE NEWSPAPER GAINED REAL PRESTIGE... SO MUCH SO THAT THE GOVERNMENT DECIDED TO SHUT IT DOWN...

POLITICAL JOURNALISM CAME TO LIFE WITH MARX: THE USE OF THE PRESS TO SPREAD IDEAS, TO CRITICISE BAD GOVERNMENT AND TO LET PUBLIC OPINION IN ON THE AWFUL MISERY OF THE PEOPLE...

MARX WAS TRYING TO PUT INTO PRACTICE (AND INTO THE HEADS OF HUMBLE FOLK) THE IDEAS WHICH CAFÉ PHILOSOPHERS ONLY TALKED ABOUT.

MARX INVENTED DOCUMENTARY REPORTING WITH HIS ARTICLES ON THE PEASANTS OF THE MOSELLE DISTRICT...

YES, EVEN CHARLIE MARX HAD FEELINGS... AT THE TENDER AGE OF 18 HE WAS ALREADY COURTING A BEAUTIFUL—AND RICH—GERMAN GIRL, JENNY VON WESTPHALEN, A YOUNG ARISTOCRAT, AND THIS CAUSED HER FATHER SERIOUS WORRIES ABOUT HER FUTURE...

IN PARIS, MARX WORKED ON ALL THE ISSUES PUBLISHED BY THE MAGAZINE "FRANCO-GERMAN ANNALS"...

WORSE, THIS MAGAZINE WHICH WAS MEANT FOR UNDERGROUND DISTRIBUTION IN GERMANY CAUSED HIM LOTS OF PROBLEMS... BESIDES, HE DIDN'T GET ALONG WITH THE DIRECTOR, RUGE, WHOSE VIEWS MARX DIDN'T SHARE, AND WHO CALLED MARX "REALLY MULE-HEADED"...

WHY?
BECAUSE IN PARIS, MARX HAD GROWN EVEN MORE RADICAL AS A DIRECT RESULT OF HIS CONTACT WITH FRENCH IDEAS (BLANC-PROUDHON-LEROUX) AND THE RUSSIAN ANARCHISTS BOTKIN AND BAKUNIN...
(AND MEANWHILE HE STARTED STUDYING THE ECONOMIC THEORIES OF THE ENGLISHMEN, ADAM SMITH AND DAVID RICARDO)...

PROUDHON
FRENCH PHILOSOPHER

BUT THE GREATEST EFFECT ON MARX WAS HIS FRIENDSHIP WITH ANOTHER FELLOW-GERMAN, FREDERICK ENGELS, WHOM HE'D MET IN THE "RHENISH GAZETTE" DAYS

WHO IS ENGELS?

ENGELS—THREE YEARS YOUNGER THAN MARX—THE SON OF A RICH TEXTILE MANUFACTURER, WAS SENT TO ENGLAND TO RUN ONE OF HIS FATHER'S BRANCHES THERE. ENGELS WAS QUITE RESTLESS ANYWAY, BUT FIRST-HAND CONTACT WITH WORKING CLASS MISERY AFFECTED HIM DEEPLY...

MANY ARTISTS OF THE TIME HAVE LEFT US EVIDENCE OF THE TERRIBLE EXPLOITATION SUFFERED BY ENGLISH WORKERS...

BECAUSE OF THEIR SMALL SIZE (AND LITTLENESS OF THEIR WAGES) CHILDREN WERE EXPLOITED IN MINES AND OTHER KINDS OF INDUSTRY BY INHUMAN BOSSES...

The Swine!!

FROM ENGLAND, ENGELS WROTE AN ARTICLE FOR THE "ANNALS" DESCRIBING THE CONDITION OF THE WORKING CLASS THERE. MARX WAS POWERFULLY STRUCK BY IT.
THEY BECAME CLOSE FRIENDS DURING A PARIS VISIT AND DECIDED TO WORK TOGETHER...

BEFORE SEEKING REFUGE IN LONDON, MARX AND ENGELS HAD TAKEN PART IN A SECRET SOCIETY CALLED THE "COMMUNIST LEAGUE" WHICH COMMISSIONED THEM TO PREPARE THE NOW FAMOUS

COMMUNIST MANIFESTO

AT FIRST IT DIDN'T CAUSE ANY GREAT SENSATION. BUT LATER, BIT BY BIT, IT BEGAN TO CREATE REAL WORLD-WIDE ANXIETY. THE MANIFESTO'S PUBLICATION TURNS OUT TO BE ONE OF THE MORE IMPORTANT EVENTS IN HUMAN HISTORY...

"A spectre is haunting Europe – the specrre of Communism. All the powers of old Europe have entered into a holy alliance to exorcise the spectre: Pope and Czar, Metternich and Guizot, French Radicals and German police-spies. Where is the party in opposition that has not been decried as communistic by its opponents in power? Where the Opposition that has not hurled back the branding reproach..."

(so it begins: but more of that later...)

ENGELS HELPED OUT AND OFTEN HAD TO SUPPORT HIM. THE LITTLE INHERITANCE MARX RECEIVED WHEN HIS FATHER-IN-LAW DIED WENT TO PAY OFF HIS DEBTS. A JOB IN A RAILWAY OFFICE HE WAS ABOUT TO GET WAS REFUSED HIM BECAUSE OF HIS TERRIBLE HANDWRITING...

(Judge for yourself..!)

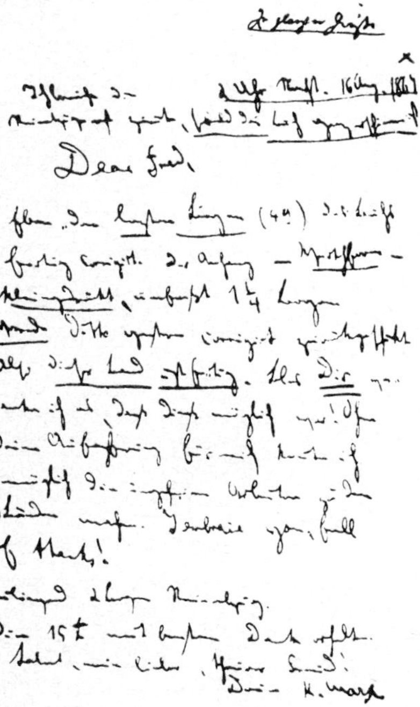

MARX NEVER HAD A STEADY INCOME OR A PERMANENT JOB OR A BANK ACCOUNT... BUT WHAT HE COULDN'T EARN FOR HIS OWN FAMILY, HE WON FOR MILLIONS OF OTHERS THROUGH HIS WRITINGS...

DON'T IMAGINE THAT CHARLIE'S IDEAS WERE GREETED WITH WILD ENTHUSIASM BY THE PUBLIC. ON THE CONTRARY – NO ONE KNEW ANYTHING ABOUT MARX OUTSIDE A SMALL CIRCLE OF GERMAN EXILES AND A FEW INTELLECTUALS...

Marx's economic theories made no immediate impact on the debate inside the workers' movement or on other thinkers, except after his death (1883). This is true of his theories on value and surplus value, accumulation, exploitation, pauperization, crisis and appropriation, class struggle and revolution. But by the end of the century, several such theories were being hotly discussed within the workers' movement; while others were gradually accepted as absolutely valid.

THE NUMBERS OF HIS BOOKS AND REVIEW ARTICLES PRINTED WERE VERY SMALL. COMRADE MARX'S STYLE WASN'T TERRIBLY CLEAR, AND SO, VERY FEW WERE ABLE TO GRASP HIS DARING AND COMPLEX IDEAS.

IN FACT, IT WAS ONLY IN 1917, WITH LENIN'S VICTORY IN RUSSIA, THAT THE WORKS OF MARX WERE HEARD OF THROUGHOUT THE WORLD, AND STUDIED AND DISCUSSED...

Working in misery was not easy, and the Marx family of six became ever more proletarian in character during those London years. Sometimes Marx could not go out because his clothes were at the pawnbroker's. Even paper to write on was lacking, as well as the necessities for his family. During this Dean Street period, 1851, a daughter, Francesca, was born only to die in a year.

Jenny Marx describes the hard times in a letter to a friend: "Our three children lay down by us and we all wept for the little angel whose livid, lifeless body was in the next room. Our beloved child's death occurred at the time of the hardest privation, our German friends being unable to help us just then. . . Anguish in my heart, I hurried to a French emigrant who lived not far away and used to come to see us, and begged him to help us in our terrible necessity. He immediately gave me two pounds with the most friendly sympathy. That money was used to pay for a coffin in which my child now rests in peace. She had no cradle when she came into the world and for a long time was refused a last resting place. . ."

THE LAST 25 YEARS OF MARX'S LIFE WERE SPENT WORKING ON HIS MAJOR WORK:

'CAPITAL'

Das Kapital.

Kritik der politischen Oekonomie.

Von

Karl Marx.

Erster Band.

Buch I: Der Produktionsprocess des Kapitals.

Das Recht der Uebersetzung wird vorbehalten.

Hamburg

Verlag von Otto Meissner.

1867.

New-York: L. W. Schmidt. 24 Barclay-Street.

WHICH HE DIDN'T MANAGE TO FINISH.

ONLY THE FIRST OF THE THREE VOLUMES HE HAD PLANNED WAS ENTIRELY COMPLETED BY HIM. THE OTHER TWO WERE PUT INTO ORDER AND FINISHED, ACCORDING TO MARX'S NOTES, BY ENGELS.

MARX'S LAST YEARS WERE FILLED WITH ILLNESS AND INFIRMITIES...

ASIDE FROM ALL THE ARTICLES HE WROTE FOR GERMAN, ENGLISH, FRENCH AND AMERICAN JOURNALS, MARX PRODUCED THE FOLLOWING BOOKS:

1841: On the Difference Between the Natural Philosophy of Democritus and Epicurus

1843: On the Jewish Question

1844: The Critique of Hegel's Philosophy of Right (and) Economic and Philosophic Manuscripts

1845: The Holy Family (and) The Poverty of Philosophy

1846: The German Ideology

1848: The Communist Manifesto

1850: Class Struggles in France

1852: The 18th. Brumaire of Louis Bonaparte

1857: A Contribution to the Critique of Political Economy

1865: Value, Price and Profit

1871: The Civil War in France

1867, 1893, 1894: Capital Volumes I, II and III

MARX'S WORKS ARE CONSIDERED THE WORKING CLASS BIBLE. YET IT'S ODD HOW VERY FEW WORKERS UNDERSTAND WHAT HE'S WRITTEN. MOST OF WHAT HE WROTE IS ABSTRACT, AS DIFFICULT AS MATHEMATICS, BUT IT DID CHANGE THE WORLD...

EVERY SOCIAL MOVEMENT OVER THE LAST 100 YEARS HAS BEEN INFLUENCED BY MARX (CUBA, CHILE, MEXICO, VIETNAM, KOREA, CYPRUS, HUNGARY, CZECHOSLOVAKIA, INDONESIA, POLAND, TIBET, BOLIVIA, GUATEMALA, CONGO, ALBANIA, GREECE, ANGOLA, EAST GERMANY, ETC, ETC.

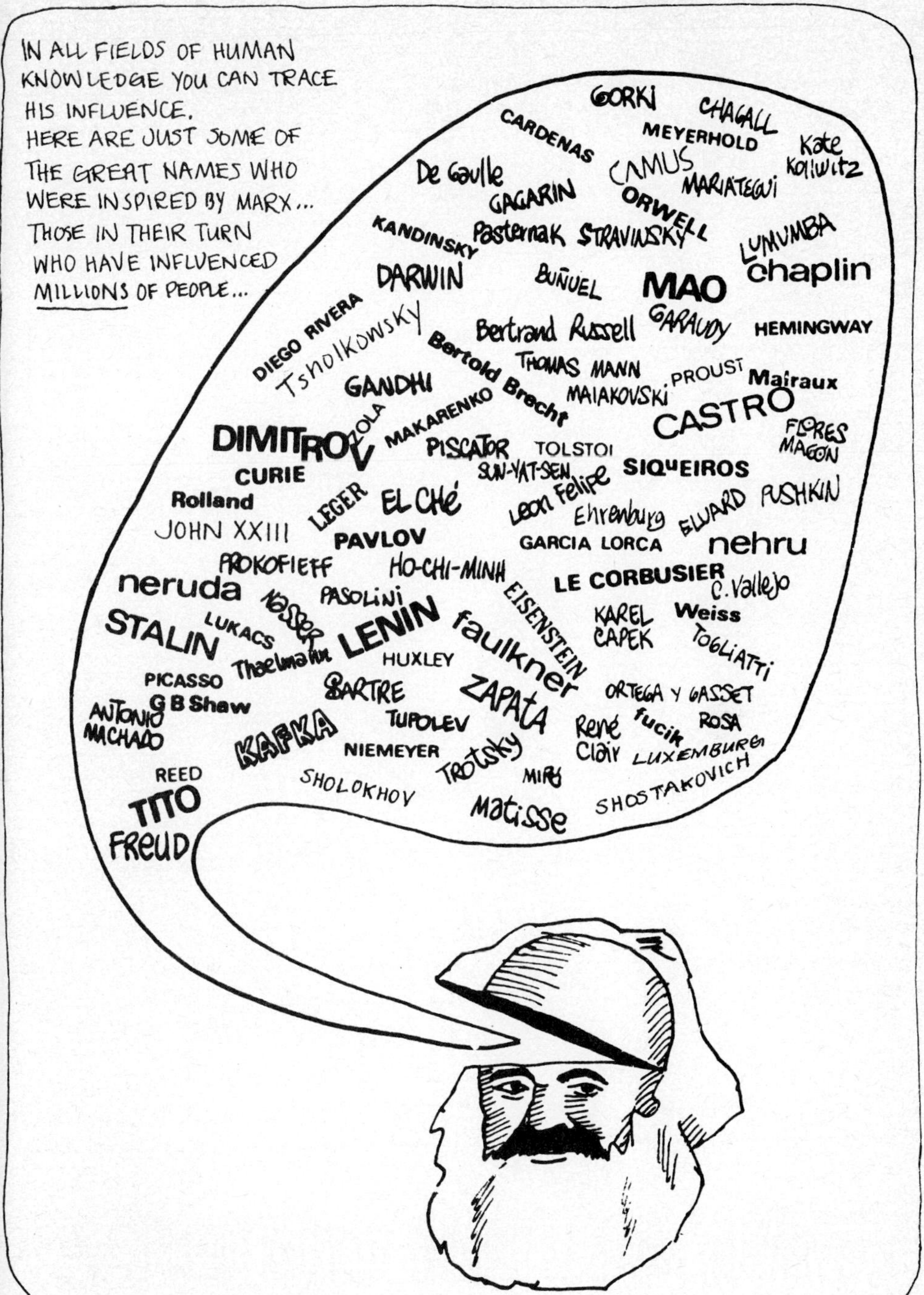
IN ALL FIELDS OF HUMAN KNOWLEDGE YOU CAN TRACE HIS INFLUENCE.
HERE ARE JUST SOME OF THE GREAT NAMES WHO WERE INSPIRED BY MARX... THOSE IN THEIR TURN WHO HAVE INFLUENCED MILLIONS OF PEOPLE...
GORKI
CHAGALL
CARDENAS
MEYERHOLD
Kate Kollwitz
De Gaulle
CAMUS
MARIATEGUI
GAGARIN
ORWELL
KANDINSKY
Pasternak
STRAVINSKY
LUMUMBA
chaplin
DARWIN
BUÑUEL
MAO
DIEGO RIVERA
Tsiolkowsky
Bertrand Russell
GARAUDY
HEMINGWAY
Bertold Brecht
THOMAS MANN
PROUST
Malraux
GANDHI
MAIAKOVSKI
CASTRO
ZOLA
MAKARENKO
FLORES MAGON
DIMITROV
PISCATOR
TOLSTOI
CURIE
SUN-YAT-SEN
SIQUEIROS
Rolland
LEGER
EL CHÉ
Leon Felipe
Ehrenburg
ELUARD
PUSHKIN
JOHN XXIII
PAVLOV
GARCIA LORCA
nehru
PROKOFIEFF
HO-CHI-MINH
LE CORBUSIER
C. Vallejo
neruda
NASSER
PASOLINI
EISENSTEIN
KAREL CAPEK
Weiss
STALIN
LUKACS
LENIN
faulkner
TOGLIATTI
Thaelmann
HUXLEY
PICASSO
SARTRE
ZAPATA
ORTEGA Y GASSET
G B Shaw
ANTONIO MACHADO
TUPOLEV
René Clair
fucik
ROSA LUXEMBURG
KAFKA
NIEMEYER
Trotsky
REED
SHOLOKHOV
MIRO
SHOSTAKOVICH
TITO
Matisse
FREUD

SO, AFTER THIS SHORT BIOGRAPHY OF THE MAN, LET'S GO ON TO SEE WHAT MARXISM IS, AND HOW CHARLES MARX ACTUALLY MANAGED TO CONTRIBUTE SO MUCH TO HUMANITY, LIKE IT OR NOT...
To do that, we'll have to go back in time and seek the roots of Marxism...
...WHAT HAS MAN BEEN THINKING THROUGH THE AGES ?

IT'S NOT POSSIBLE TO GUESS WHAT MEN THINK IF THEY DON'T EXPRESS IT... EVEN LESS IF THEY LACKED THE MEANS TO WRITE DOWN WHAT WAS SAID...

WHAT DID THE FIRST HUMANS THINK?

IN THE BEGINNING, IGNORANCE AND FEAR PREDOMINATED. BECAUSE THEY DIDN'T KNOW THE MEANINGS OF THINGS, EARLY PEOPLES WERE AFRAID OF EVERYTHING WHICH MOVED, AND THEIR FIRST THOUGHT WAS ABOUT THE SUPERNATURAL: WHO MADE THE NOISE OF THUNDER? WHO MOVED THE EARTH? WHO MADE IT RAIN?

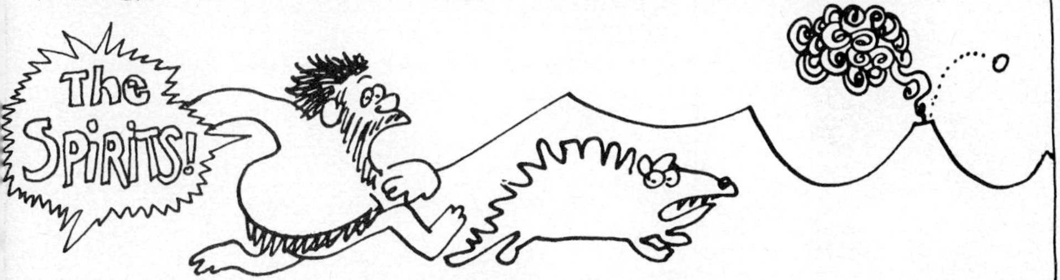

THAT'S WHY, TO PROVIDE SOME KIND OF EXPLANATION FOR NATURAL EVENTS, MANKIND CREATED THE GODS: THE GOD OF RAIN, OF FIRE, OF EARTH, OF SUN, THE GODDESS OF FERTILITY, THE GOD OF HUNTING...

OUT OF THIS CAME THE MAGICIANS AND SORCERERS WHO EXPLOITED THE "IDEA OF DIVINITY" FOR THEIR OWN BENEFIT. BY USING ALL KINDS OF CHEAP TRICKS THEY PASSED THEMSELVES OFF AS SPECIAL "DELEGATES" OF THE GODS WITH FANTASTIC POWERS...

THIS IS THE WAY GRADUALLY AN "UPPER" CLASS WAS FORMED- OR A *RULING CLASS*– AND A LOWER - OR *RULED* - CLASS... THOSE WHO LET THEMSELVES BE EXPLOITED AND THOSE WHO LEAD FOOLS BY THE NOSE (AND AVOID WORK...)

EVEN SO, SOME BEGAN TO USE THEIR HEADS TO FIND LOGICAL EXPLANATIONS FOR THE PHENOMENA OF NATURE: THE "THINKERS"...

PHILOSOPHY STARTED AS CRITICISM OF RELIGIOUS BELIEFS. BY SEEKING LOGICAL REASONS FOR THE THINGS IN NATURE, MANKIND CREATED THE SCIENCE OF PHILOSOPHY...*

TWO OPPOSED CAMPS SPRANG UP WHICH STILL PERSIST TO THIS DAY:
RELIGION ON ONE SIDE, SCIENCE ON THE OTHER...

ONE OF THE VERY FIRST PHILOSOPHERS WE HEAR OF, A GREEK BY THE NAME OF XENOPHANES OF COLOPHON, REFUSED TO ADORE IDOLS, BECAUSE, AS HE SAID:

THE IDEAS OF XENOPHANES GOT ROUND, BUT THE RULING CLASS WASN'T GOING TO TOLERATE RIDICULE OR DOUBT ABOUT THE EXISTENCE OF THE GODS WHICH SUPPORTED THEIR "SACRED AND LEGITIMATE" CLAIMS TO POWER...
BUT STILL MANY LISTENED TO HIM...

AS TIME WENT ON – AND PROFITS ROSE – THE RULING CLASS PERFECTED ITS RELIGION AND ADDED MORE GODS, MORE MYTHS, MORE RITES AND CEREMONIES. TEMPLES WERE BUILT IN WHICH GODS AND GODDESSES WERE WORSHIPPED, WHICH USUALLY MEANT "DONATIONS" OF MONEY OR OTHER THINGS HAD TO BE PAID UP "TO ATTRACT DIVINE FAVOURS"...

AT THE SAME TIME, A "DIVINE CASTE" SET ITSELF APART. WITCH DOCTORS HAD ELEVATED THEMSELVES TO THE PRIESTHOOD. THEIR POWER WAS SO GREAT THAT, TOGETHER WITH KINGS AND PHARAOHS, THEY CREATED HUGE EMPIRES OF FAITHFUL SLAVES "BY THE WILL OF THE SUPREME GODS"...

The whole business went so far that kings too wanted to be worshipped as gods...

THE STATE COMMANDED WHICH GODS COULD BE WORSHIPPED OR NOT...

EVEN RELIGION HAD TO INVENT SOME KIND OF SCIENCE FOR ITSELF (*THEOLOGY = THE PHILOSOPHY OF DIVINITY*) TO JUSTIFY ITS EXISTENCE.

THE FIRST THING RELIGION INVENTED WAS A FAITH IN THE "BEYOND", THE <u>AFTER LIFE</u>...

THE EGYPTIANS

THE EGYPTIAN ARGUMENT WAS QUITE SIMPLE: MEN WERE CREATED BY OSIRIS AND MUST OBEY HIS WILL ON THIS EARTH.
THEY MUST PUT UP WITH SLAVERY IN THE HOPE THAT, IF THEY BEHAVE WELL, A BETTER *AFTER*-LIFE AWAITS THEM IN THE NEXT WORLD – NO MORE SLAVERY, ONLY ETERNAL BLISS...

SOUNDS PRETTY FAMILIAR, DOESN'T IT?

HOWEVER, THE WORLD WASN'T TOTALLY DEPRIVED OF MEN (NO MATTER HOW FEW) ABLE TO RESIST BLIND FAITH, WHO PREFER TO COME TO THEIR OWN CONCLUSIONS, RELYING ON SCIENCE...

THALES

OF MILETUS IS CONSIDERED THE FATHER OF PHILOSOPHY. HE LIVED FOUR CENTURIES BEFORE CHRIST AND DEVOTED HIMSELF TO ASTRONOMY AND SCIENTIFIC ENQUIRY INTO NATURE...

Pythagoras

–ANOTHER FAMOUS PAIR OF WHISKERS – FATHER OF MATHEMATICS – CONCLUDED THAT NUMBER STANDS AT THE ORIGIN OF ALL THINGS, AND THEREFORE LIFE IS...

PYTHAGORAS AND HIS FOLLOWERS (HE FOUNDED A PECULIAR SECT WHICH PROHIBITED THE EATING OF BEANS!!) WERE THE FIRST TO DECLARE THAT THE EARTH ISN'T AT THE CENTRE OF THE UNIVERSE...

AS A RESULT, THEY WERE PERSECUTED AND THE PYTHAGOREAN COMMUNITY WAS SCATTERED BY RELIGIOUS FANATICS...

NEXT CAME **HERACLITUS**, OFTEN NAMED THE FATHER OF DIALECTICS, THAT IS, THE ART OF ARGUMENT...

HERACLITUS, AN ATHEIST PHILOSOPHER, USED TO TEACH THAT EVERYTHING EXISTS AND AT THE SAME TIME DOESN'T EXIST... THAT ALL THINGS ARE IN MOTION AND FLUID CHANGE, CONTINUOUSLY APPEARING AND DISAPPEARING...

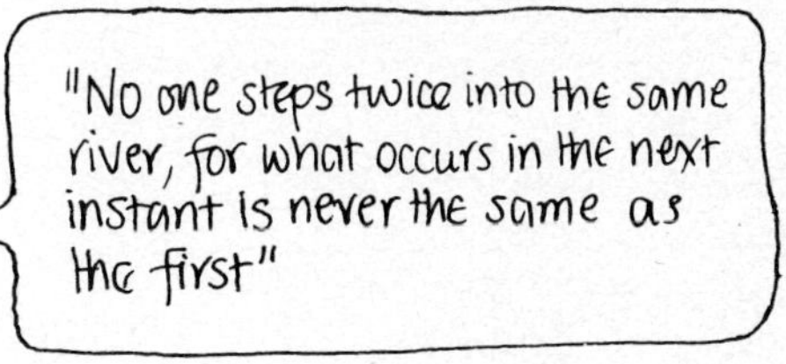

MORE OFTEN THAN NOT, THESE ENLIGHTENED FELLOWS WERE PERSECUTED AND ENDED UP BADLY. SCIENCE WAS FAR TOO BACKWARD AND IT WASN'T THE TIME TO TEST NEW "ATHEIST THEORIES"...

AND NOW WE'RE OFF TO SICILY...

AT AGRIGENTUM, EMPEDOCLES, ANOTHER PHILOSOPHER, USED TO CLAIM THAT HUMANS WERE ONCE UPON A TIME DESCENDED FROM GODS, BUT HAD BEEN CAST DOWN TO EARTH BECAUSE OF THEIR WICKEDNESS AND IMPURITY...

HE ALSO THOUGHT THAT EVERYTHING WAS MADE UP OF FIRE, AIR, EARTH AND WATER – A THEORY THAT SURVIVED RIGHT INTO THE MIDDLE AGES...

THESE FOUR ELEMENTS, SAID HE, WERE INFLUENCED BY TWO FORCES; ATTRACTION AND REPULSION, LOVE AND HATE, WHICH EXPLAINS HOW ALL THINGS IN THE UNIVERSE CHANGE ACCORDING TO THE RHYTHMS OF LIFE AND DEATH...

HERE'S ONE MORE WHO DIED FOR HIS OPINIONS:

ANAXAGORAS...

AND YET HE SAID NO MORE THAN THE TRUTH: "the sun is a mass of fire and stone"... (AND NOT A GOD AS THE IGNORANT ATHENIANS BELIEVED)...

Socrates

THIS GRANDADDY OF HUMOUR USED TO JOKE ABOUT EVERYTHING—ABOUT GODS, PHILOSOPHERS, GOVERNMENTS, RELIGION... AND ALSO ABOUT HIMSELF. AND IT'S TRUE HE WAS NO BEAUTY... SHORT, FAT, BALD WRINKLED, AND REALLY UNTIDY...

THIS WAS ONE OF HIS MOST ORIGINAL DISCOVERIES: HE DENIED MORALITY AS A SYNONYM FOR RELIGION... AND HERE'S HOW:

IN THE END, SOCRATES WAS ACCUSED OF CORRUPTING THE YOUTH, OF ATTACKING INSTITUTIONS, OF ATHEISM, LACK OF MORALS AND SO ON AND SO ON.

OF COURSE, THIS MEANT THE DEATH PENALTY, WHICH HE ACCEPTED BY DRINKING POISONOUS HEMLOCK FROM A BIG CUP.

BUT, IN BETWEEN SIPS, HE WENT ON TALKING CALMLY TO HIS DISCIPLES...

GREEK PHILOSOPHY ENDS WITH THESE THREE GIANTS:

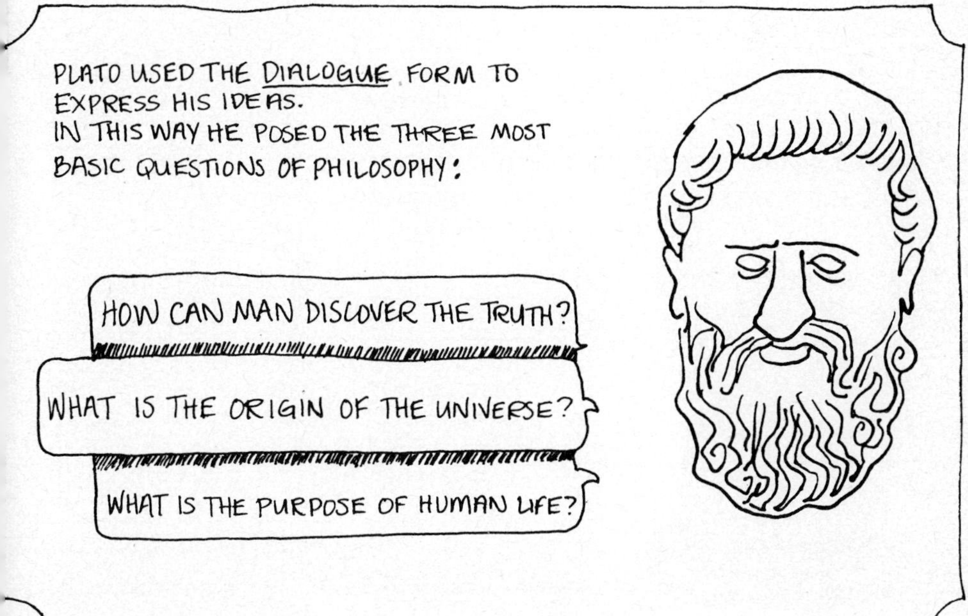

TRUE KNOWLEDGE OF THINGS – SAYS PLATO – COMES NEITHER THROUGH PERCEPTION NOR REASON... OR, THAT IS, MAN CANNOT KNOW TRUTH BY MEANS OF SCIENCE BUT ONLY THROUGH "INSPIRATION" ARRIVING FROM THE BEYOND. MAN CANNOT KNOW THINGS ON HIS OWN, BUT ONLY BY THE IDEAS GOD GIVES HIM OF THINGS...

HIS INTERPRETATIONS OF REALITY WERE SURE TO PLEASE THE AUTHORITIES:
E.G. THAT HUMBLER FOLK SHOULD SERVE THOSE RICHER AND NOBLER THAN THEY.
THAT THE POOR SHOULDN'T WORRY ABOUT THEIR FATE SINCE THEY WILL BE HAPPY IN THE NEXT WORLD — THE ONE TO COME, OF COURSE, NOT THIS ONE WHICH IS JUST IMAGINARY ANYWAY...

LATER ON, IT'S WELL KNOWN, PLATO'S IDEAS WERE USED TO PROP UP THE DOCTRINE OF THE "IMMORTALITY" OF THE SOUL AND THE SINFUL NATURE OF THE FLESH — THAT IS, OF MATTER.

amen!

DEMOCRITUS

INSTEAD WAS PERSECUTED FOR UPHOLDING "MATERIALIST" IDEAS...

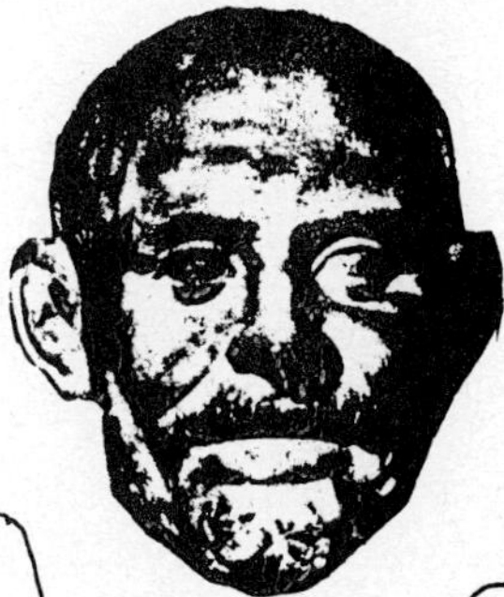

"Cosmic substance is made up of an infinite number of elements or particles physically invisible, indestructible and infinite, which vary in size and shape, and are in eternal motion"...

DEMROCRITUS WAS TALKING ABOUT

ATOMS

FOUR CENTURIES BEFORE CHRIST AND TWENTY FOUR BEFORE EINSTEIN!

THE GREEK EPOCH CLOSES WITH

ARISTOTLE

A REAL MASTER-MIND; A PROTÉGÉ OF ALEXANDER THE GREAT, A GENIUS IN ALL FIELDS OF HUMAN ENQUIRY (HE WROTE ON PHYSICS, METAPHYSICS, ETHICS, POLITICS, PHILOSOPHY, BIOLOGY, ZOOLOGY...) A REMARKABLE TEACHER AND A TIRELESS SCIENTIST. HIS INFLUENCE LASTED EVERWHERE UNTIL THE BIRTH OF MATERIALISM IN THE 18th. CENTURY

SO, "ARY'S-THOUGHT-ALL" WAS THE FIRST TO REALISE THAT THE ECONOMIC SET-UP GIVES RISE TO SOCIAL INEQUALITIES. THOUGH IT'S ALSO TRUE THAT HE GAVE HIS O.K. TO SLAVERY BECAUSE IT WAS "NECESSARY" TO SOCIETY...

ARISTOTLE FOUND PLATO'S IDEAS RIDICULOUS.
HE CONSIDERED THE <u>SENSES</u> AS THE ONLY SOURCES OF TRUTH.

HIS TEACHINGS ABOUT ETHICS WAS THAT THE GOAL OF LIFE WAS HAPPINESS.
SO, HE ADMITTED THAT ANYONE LUCKY ENOUGH TO HAVE <u>MONEY</u> OR <u>POWER</u> OR <u>HONOUR</u> WAS BOUND TO BE HAPPY...

THE FIRST PHILOSOPHICAL ENQUIRY WHICH THE YOUNG MARX STARTED ON, DEALS PRECISELY WITH THESE "GIANTS" OF GREEK THOUGHT.
IT WAS THE SUBJECT OF HIS Ph.D. THESIS AT UNIVERSITY

"On the Difference between the Natural Philosophy of Democritus and Epicurus..."

IF ANYONE CARES TO READ IT, (IT CAN BE FOUND IN SOME LIBRARY NEARBY) AND CAN DIGEST IT IN A FORTNIGHT, I'LL GUARANTEE HE'LL BE A REAL MASTER MIND... (OR A COMPLETE NUT-CASE IN A MONTH...)

PHILOSOPHY DOESN'T QUITE END HERE...
EVEN IF IT DID ALMOST VANISH WITH THE APPEARANCE OF THE FALSE, BACKWARD CHRISTIANITY OF THE MIDDLE AGES...

NOT BY ACCIDENT, THIS UNBELIEVABLE EPOCH IS NAMED:

THE AGE OF FAITH

(AND BY 'FAITH' UNDERSTAND THE DENIAL OF <u>ALL</u> SCIENTIFIC REASONING)

DURING THIS PERIOD, AT ROME, A FEROCIOUS DICTATORSHIP WAS SET UP WHICH DECLARED ANYONE A "HERETIC" WHO DIDN'T THINK LIKE THE CHURCH... EVERY TRACE OF PHILOSOPHY DISAPPEARS FROM EUROPE WHEN THE "HOLY INQUISITION" LIGHTS THE EXECUTION FIRES...

DURING THESE DARK TIMES, SCIENCE AND THOUGHT DID NOT DEVELOP EXCEPT OUTSIDE EUROPE, IN THE MUSLIM WORLD, WHERE MEN LIKE AVERROËS AND AVICENNA REFUTED THE BIBLE AS FALSE, OR AT BEST AS "SYMBOLIC TALES MEANT FOR IGNORANT FOLK"...

△ An illustration of 'Erasmus of Rotterdam' censored by the Spanish Inquisitors because he was a "heretic"

IN THE ABSENCE OF PROPER PHILOSOPHY, A FEW, WHO HAD NOTHING BETTER TO DO, PASSED THEIR TIME IN THEOLOGICAL QUIBBLES ABOUT WHETHER ANGELS HAD NAVELS, OR THE IMMORTALITY OF LOBSTERS, OR THE MYSTERIES OF THE HOLY TRINITY AND THE CHURCH. THOMAS OF AQUINO WAS ONE SUCH WORTHY FELLOW WHO WROTE **21 VOLUMES** OF MENTAL GYMNASTICS TO DEFEND THE DOCTRINES OF THE ROMAN CATHOLIC CHURCH...

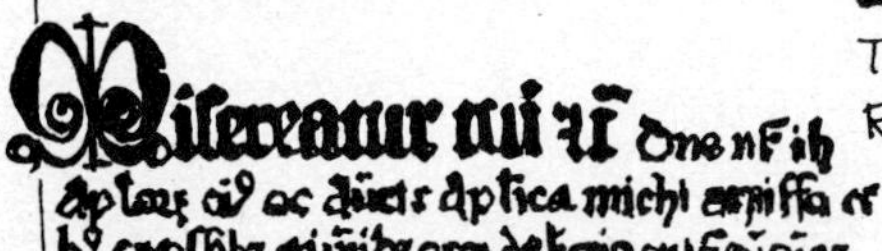

(These are still studied today in Catholic seminaries...)

MACHIAVELLI (1469-1527) WAS THE FIRST TO COME ALONG AND ATTACK THE CHURCH AND PREACH REBELLION AGAINST THE DICTATORSHIP OF THE CLERGY...

NOW BEGINS THE

RENAISSANCE

WHICH IS TO SAY – THE ALL-OUT COUNTER-ATTACK OF REASON AND SCIENCE AGAINST DOGMA, RELIGIOUS TYRANNY AND FANATICISM: AND IT SCORED AN IMPORTANT VICTORY FOR HUMANITY, THAT IS, FREEDOM OF THOUGHT...

BACON

THIS IS THE PERIOD IN HUMAN HISTORY WHEN FIRST-RATE MINDS SUDDENLY FLOWERED. PROOF OF THE VICTORY OF MIND OVER DARKNESS: DANTE, PETRARCH, DAVINCI, ERASMUS, LUTHER, VICO, COPERNICUS, GALILEO, KEPLER, NEWTON, BACON AND GIORDANO BRUNO...

Giordano Bruno (c.1548-1600), a Dominican monk and Galileo's contemporary, renounced obedience to his Order to follow the Pantheistic doctrine whereby God and Nature are considered as the active and passive elements of reality. Prisoner of the Inquisition, he refused to recant and was burned alive at the stake in 1600.

ALL OF THEM ARE GUIDED BY ONE IDEA: SEEK THE TRUTH INDEPENDENTLY OF THE CHURCH AND RELIGION.
BUT EACH ONE STAGGERED UNDER THE HEAVY YOKE IMPOSED BY THE CHURCH...

THE IDEA ISN'T ESPECIALLY REMARKABLE IN ITSELF, EXCEPT FOR TWO DETAILS: ONE, THAT VICO MAINTAINED IT DESPITE THE FEUDAL SOCIETY AROUND HIM, AND TWO, THAT HE SPOKE FOR THE FIRST TIME OF AN EVOLUTION OF SOCIETY TOWARDS DEMOCRACY THROUGH CLASS-STRUGGLE...

CERTAINLY, HIS MISTAKE WAS TO END HIS EVOLUTION HERE AND ASSUME THE BOURGEOIS STATE WOULDN'T BE CHANGED FOR THE BETTER, BUT ONLY THAT HISTORY WOULD START ALL OVER AGAIN FROM A FIRST PHASE ON A NEW CYCLE OF EVOLUTION...

DESCARTES & SPINOZA

WERE THE NEXT GREAT ADEPTS OF PHILOSOPHY IN THE XVII CENTURY, A TIME STILL DOMINATED BY THE CHURCH OF ROME...

POSSESSED OF A TRULY SCIENTIFIC SPIRIT, RENÉ DESCARTES WRESTLED HARD TO EXPLAIN THINGS FROM A MATERIALISTIC POINT OF VIEW, REASONING ABOUT THE NATURE OF THINGS, AND AT THE SAME TIME TRYING TO PROVE GOD'S EXISTENCE...

"All things we can conceive of clearly and distinctly, exist..."

THE CARTESIAN SYSTEM ("I THINK, THEREFORE I AM") WAS PART MATERIALIST, PART IDEALIST. HE BELIEVED THE HUMAN BEING WAS ONLY A MACHINE, BUT WITH A SOUL... AND HE EVEN LOCATED IT SPECIFICALLY: THE SOUL WAS HIDDEN IN THE PINEAL GLAND INSIDE THE BRAIN...

DESCARTES INTRODUCES US TO A MECHANISTIC CONCEPT OF THE WORLD. LATER WE'LL SEE WHAT THIS IS AND WHETHER IT'S EDIBLE...

SPINOZA LIVED A LONELY LIFE, FIRST BECAUSE HE WAS A JEW, AND SECOND BECAUSE HE STOPPED BEING ONE AND TURNED ATHEIST... SPINOZA PROCLAIMED SOMETHING COMPLETELY UNTHINKABLE IN THOSE DAYS:

GOD DOESN'T EXIST IN THE WAY RELIGION PREACHES, BUT—SPINOZA AFFIRMED—ONLY AS AN IMPERSONAL AND SPIRITUAL "PRINCIPLE", AS A SUBSTANCE WHICH CONSTITUTES THE REALITY OF THE UNIVERSE... (PANTHEISM BELIEVES EVERYTHING IS GOD). THAT'S WHY SPINOZA LIVED IN POVERTY, POLISHING EYE-GLASS LENSES FOR A LIVING...

BUT ALL THESE SEMI-ATHEIST, MATERIALIST PHILOSOPHERS HAD ONE FLAW: THEY PLACED TOO MUCH CONFIDENCE IN SCIENCE. THEY STARTED FROM THE ASSUMPTION THAT MAN IS PART OF NATURE (TRUE) AND THAT HUMAN RELATIONS ARE REGULATED BY THE SAME LAW WHICH APPLIES TO ALL OTHER NATURAL EVENTS (FALSE)

BECAUSE DESCARTES AND SPINOZA AND THEIR FOLLOWERS WERE WRONG TO BELIEVE THAT NATURE DOESN'T CHANGE, DOESN'T EVOLVE, AND THAT IT OBEYS ONLY ETERNAL AND UNCHANGING LAWS.

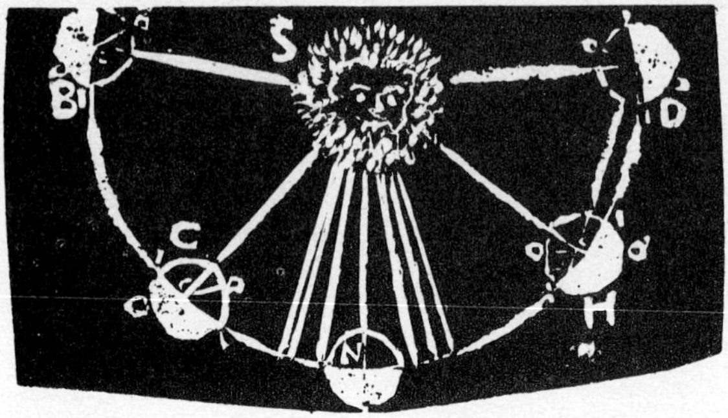

DIDEROT (AMONG OTHERS) CAME TO THE CONCLUSION THAT THE UNIVERSE AND HUMANITY HAD ALWAYS BEEN THE SAME. NEITHER HAD EVER UNDERGONE EVOLUTIONS, BUT BOTH WENT ON REPEATING THEMSELVES IN THE SAME CYCLES OF LIFE AND DEATH...

IN THEIR EYES, THE PEOPLE HAD NO EXISTENCE. ONLY "HEROES" EXISTED (KINGS, CAPTAINS, PROPHETS AND PHILOSOPHERS) WHO ACTED AS LEADERS. THESE WERE THE "DRIVING FORCE" OF HISTORY. CLEOPATRA'S NOSE - *OR HER BEHIND* - HAD MORE EFFECT ON HISTORY THAN ALL THE PEOPLE OF EGYPT PUT TOGETHER...

TO CONTINUE WITH THE PHILOSOPHY BEFORE MARX, WE RUN ACROSS THE

EMPIRICISM OF LOCKE, BERKELEY AND HUME

LOCKE (JOHN),

AN ENGLISHMAN WHO OPPOSED THE "DIVINE RIGHT" OF KINGS, THE INFALLIBILITY (ABSOLUTE TRUTH) OF RELIGION AND THE DOGMAS OF THE CHURCH... HE'S ALSO ANOTHER MATERIALIST-ATHEIST...

LOCKE HAD THE IDEA THAT MEN WERE FREE TO THINK OF GOD IN THEIR OWN WAY, NOT AS ANY RELIGION TOLD THEM TO... THIS WAS A BIG BRICK ON THE HEADS OF PRIESTS, AND AN IDEALIST PHILOSOPHER, GEORGE BERKELEY, AN ANGLICAN BISHOP, TRIED TO REFUTE LOCKE'S THEORIES, BUT DIDN'T SUCCEED BECAUSE ANOTHER PHILOSOPHER CAME TO HIS DEFENCE...

...AGNOSTIC PHILOSOPHER (BEING SOMEONE WHO DEFENDS THE IDEA THAT NOTHING IS CERTAIN). HUME SCANDALIZED ALL OF BRITAIN WITH HIS ANTI-RELIGIOUS IDEAS, AND SO HE HAD TO PACK UP FOR FRANCE, WHICH RECEIVED HIM A LOT MORE WARMLY...

FRANCE WAS A REAL HIVE OF THE MOST ADVANCED IDEAS. A WIDESPREAD REBELLION HAD BROKEN OUT AGAINST THE TYRANNY OF THE CLERGY AND THE MONARCHY WHICH FINALLY CULMINATED IN THE FRENCH REVOLUTION AND THE TRIUMPH OF

REASON

OVER RELIGION

OF COURSE, THE FRENCH REVOLUTION DID MORE TO SPREAD POLITICAL IDEAS (SUCH AS LIBERTY, EQUALITY AND FRATERNITY) THAN PHILOSOPHICAL ONES. FOLLOWING ITS EXAMPLE, OTHER PARTS OF AMERICA FOUGHT TO FREE THEMSELVES FROM EUROPE... AND EUROPE FROM THE POPE...

(and with this liberation came the flowering of new sciences...)

AS THE EXACT OPPOSITE OF 17th CENTURY MATERIALIST PHILOSOPHY, AN IDEALIST VARIETY NOW AROSE, AND ITS GREAT CHAMPION WAS IMMANUEL
KANT
(GERMAN, 1724-1804)
Critik der reinen Vernunft von Immanuel Kant
Riga, verlegts Johann Friedrich Hartknoch 1781.
HIS MOST TALKED ABOUT WORK IS THE "CRITIQUE OF PURE REASON" WHICH COST HIM 15 YEARS OF CRITICAL ANALYSIS OF HUMAN THOUGHT. AMONG THE MANY OTHER COMPLEX POINTS BROUGHT UP IN HIS STUDY, KANT MAKES THESE:
"Every intent, whether scientific or religious, to define reality is nothing other than pure hypothesis..."
"Every attempt to apprehend transcendental knowledge is vain, since for every thesis the mind produces, one can oppose an equally valid anti-thesis..."
"It is impossible to prove the existence of God through any normal means..."
KANT WAS CERTAIN THAT THERE CANNOT BE MORALITY WITHOUT SOME BELIEF IN GOD OR IMMORTALITY, AND SO THIS OBLIGED ONE TO PRESUPPOSE THE EXISTENCE OF GOD AS A NECESSITY...

(IF WHAT WE'VE SAID SO FAR ISN'T CLEAR, DON'T WORRY. THIS HAPPENED IN THE DAYS OF "PURE" PHILOSOPHY WHICH NO ONE UNDERSTOOD OR TOOK ANY NOTICE OF EITHER...)

THE POINT OF OUR JOURNEY HAS BEEN TO ARRIVE HERE — AT GERMAN IDEALIST PHILOSOPHY, SINCE THIS WAS ALSO MARX'S STARTING POINT. SCHELLING, FICHTE AND HEGEL WERE ITS CHIEF EXPONENTS. BECAUSE OF THEM, PHILOSOPHY MAKES A GREAT LEAP FORWARD AND RECOVERS THE BEST OF GREEK PHILOSOPHY — THE DIALECTIC OR THE IDEA OF HUMAN DEVELOPMENT...

RIGHT!
MARX ALSO THOUGHT SO.
PHILOSOPHY HAD BECOME A STRAIGHTJACKET OF JARGON AND MUDDLES, IMPOSSIBLE TO MAKE OUT HEADS OR TAILS.
MARX SET HIMSELF THE JOB OF UNRAVELLING THIS CAT'S-CRADLE AND BEGIN MAKING PHILOSOPHY INTO AN EXACT SCIENCE, WITH LESS FUZZY SUPPOSITIONS, AND SO GIVE IT THE PRACTICAL MEANS TO **TRANSFORM** THE WORLD...

"PHILOSOPHERS HAVE ONLY INTERPRETED THE WORLD, IN VARIOUS WAYS; THE POINT IS TO CHANGE IT."
(Marx: 'XI Theses on Feuerbach')
SO LET'S PROCEED...
EVERYONE IS WELCOME TO JOIN WITH CHARLIE MARX IN TRYING TO FATHOM THE WORLD HE LIVED IN AND STRUGGLED TO TRANSFORM...

"The teaching of Marx is all-powerful because it is true"...
LENIN
NATURALLY, YOU CAN'T EXPECT THIS LITTLE BOOK OF MINE TO EXPOUND ALL OF MARX'S THEORY, WHICH IS A VAST OCEAN TO SWIM IN.
THE BEST THING TO DO IS SUM UP AND DIVIDE THE BASICS OF MARXISM INTO
3
MAIN BRANCHES...
1 The Philosophy of Marx
2 The Economic Doctrine of Marx
3 The Historical Materialism of Herr Marx

AS WE'VE ALREADY SEEN, THE PHILOSOPHICAL IDEAS OF MAN ARE OF TWO KINDS:

IDEALISM STARTS BY ASSUMING THE EXISTANCE OF SUPER-NATURAL AND DIVINE FORCES...

MATERIALISM CONSIDERS THAT THERE IS NOTHING BEYOND NATURAL THINGS...

IDEALISM IMAGINES THINGS,

PRESUPPOSES THE EXISTENCE OF SPIRITS, "IDEALISES" EVERYTHING, BUT DOESN'T OFFER PROOFS FOR WHAT IT PROPOSES...

(... WHICH IS LIKE TRYING TO KNOW WHAT SUGAR TASTES LIKE WITHOUT SAMPLING IT...)

MATERIALISM, INSTEAD, DOESN'T IDEALISE, BUT SEEKS THE SCIENTIFIC EXPLANATIONS OF THINGS — INCLUDING EVEN RELIGION...

IDEALISTS EXPLAIN THINGS TO THEMSELVES THROUGH RELIGION...

MATERIALISTS EXPLAIN WHAT'S WHAT ON THE BASIS OF SCIENCE...

RIGHT AT THE START OF HIS PHILOSOPHICAL STUDIES, MARX JOINED FORCES WITH <u>MATERIALISM</u>. BUT HE DEVOTED HIS ENTIRE LIFE'S WORK TO GIVING IT MORE CONSISTENCY AND SCIENTIFIC CHARACTER...

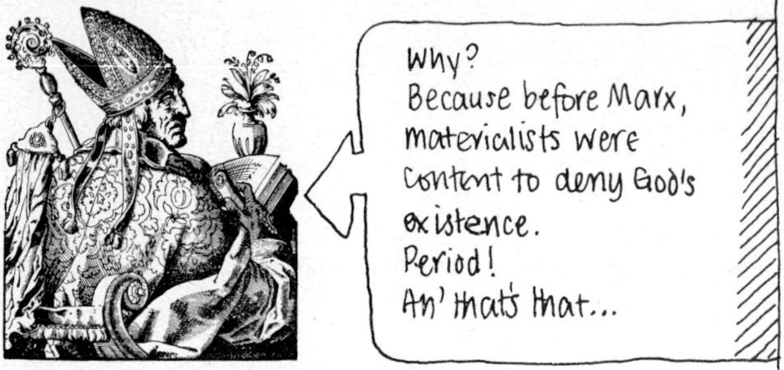

"BY GOD'S GRACE", THE MAJORITY OF ATHEISTS WISHED TO PROVE THE NON-EXISTENCE OF GOD BY STARTING THE USUAL RELIGIOUS ARGUMENTS, WHICH GOT THEM INTO USELESS MUDDLES...

IN THE <u>XVII</u> AND <u>XVIII</u> CENTURIES, THE GREATEST SCIENTIFIC DISCOVERIES WERE MADE IN THE AREAS OF THE MATHEMATICS AND <u>MECHANICS</u> OF CELESTIAL BODIES. AND SO, MATERIALISM BECAME "MECHANISTIC"...

IN OTHER WORDS, THE MATERIALIST PHILOSOPHERS EXAMINED BOTH NATURE AND SOCIAL LIFE FROM A MECHANICAL POINT OF VIEW...

BASING THEMSELVES ON MECHANICS, WHICH IN THOSE DAYS WAS THE HEIGHT OF SCIENCE, THE PHILOSOPHERS IMAGINED THAT THE SAME MECHANICAL LAWS COULD BE APPLIED AUTOMATICALLY TO LIFE AND TO NATURE...

*THIS PHILOSOPHICAL CRITERION IS CALLED METAPHYSICAL

WHY METAPHYSICAL..?

METAPHYSICS, FROM THE GREEK, "PLACED BEYOND PHYSICS".*

IN METAPHYSICS, THINGS ARE UNCHANGING (I.E. IMMUTABLE), GIVEN ONCE, AND FOR ALL, WITHOUT INTER-RELATIONSHIP, AND HENCE MAY BE EXAMINED INDEPENDENTLY, ONE FROM THE OTHER

HEGEL'S DISCIPLE, FEUERBACH REASONED LIKE THIS:

(THOSE WHO THOUGHT LIKE THIS ABOUT NATURE, COULD THINK THE SAME WAY ABOUT SOCIETY TOO. SOCIETY CHANGES VERY LITTLE FOR THE METAPHYSICIAN, EXCEPT BY REPEATING ITSELF MECHANICALLY, E.G. WARS, HUNGER, GOVERNMENTS ETC...)

*ORIGINALLY, THOSE WORKS OF ARISTOTLE PLACED AFTER HIS "PHYSICS"

HAVING RECOGNISED THE ERROR OF THE MATERIALISTS AND METAPHYSICIANS, MARX ASKED HIMSELF THE SAME QUESTION:

LET'S LEAVE GOD OUT OF IT, AND ALL THOSE WHO WANT TO DRIVE THEMSELVES CRAZY ASKING WHETHER HE EXISTS OR NOT— *SO CHARLIE SAID*— AND LET'S LOOK AT MAN AND HIS ROLE IN THE WORLD. HOW IS IT REALLY POSSIBLE THAT NOTHING CHANGES?...

INSTEAD OF THE USUAL MECHANISTIC NOTION OF NATURE AND HUMANITY, MARX AND ENGELS SET OUT A THEORY OF DEVELOPMENT —OR— A RETURN TO

DIALECTICS

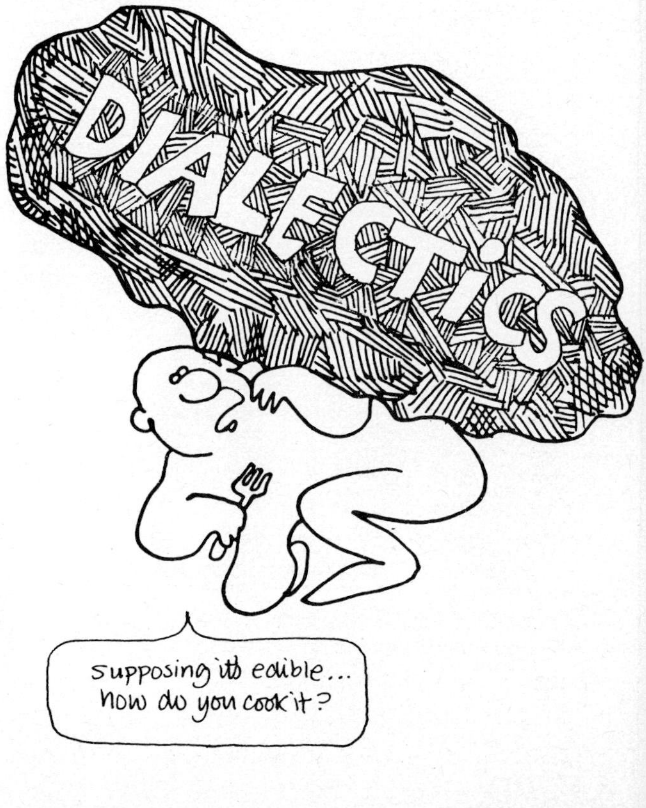

WAY BACK IN ANCIENT TIMES, SOME PHILOSOPHERS HAD ALREADY APPLIED THIS STRATEGY TO ARRIVE AT THE TRUTH, A SYSTEM OF ARGUMENT WHICH BRINGS OUT THE <u>CONTRADICTIONS</u> IN YOUR OPPONENTS' REASONING...

RELIGION (CATHOLICISM ESPECIALLY) OPPOSED DIALECTICS BECAUSE IT DIDN'T PERMIT ARGUMENT. THINGS WERE JUST AS THE BIBLE SAID—AND <u>NO</u> DISCUSSION...

KANT AND HEGEL BEGAN TO RE-EMPLOY THE DIALECTIC METHOD.
BUT HEGEL NEVER BROUGHT IT DOWN TO EARTH; AS YOU CAN SEE FROM THIS:

"... HIS HORIZON WAS FUNDAMENTALLY RESTRICTED BY THE KNOWLEDGE AND CONCEPTS CURRENT IN HIS DAY.
ONE SHOULD ADD THAT HEGEL WAS AN IDEALIST, AND FOR HIM, THE IDEAS WERE NOT MORE OR LESS ABSTRACT IMAGES OF OBJECTS; ON THE CONTRARY, THINGS AND THEIR DEVELOPMENT WERE A PROJECTION OF IDEAS WHICH HAD EXISTED, NO ONE CAN SAY HOW, EVEN BEFORE THE WORLD ITSELF EXISTED. HEGEL'S SYSTEM WAS A GIGANTIC MISCARRIAGE, BUT THE LAST OF ITS KIND. WHILE ON ONE HAND IT AFFIRMS A FORMULA ESSENTIAL TO THE CONCEPT OF HISTORY, ACCORDING TO WHICH HUMAN HISTORY IS A PROCESS OF DEVELOPMENT WHICH CANNOT, GIVEN ITS NATURE...

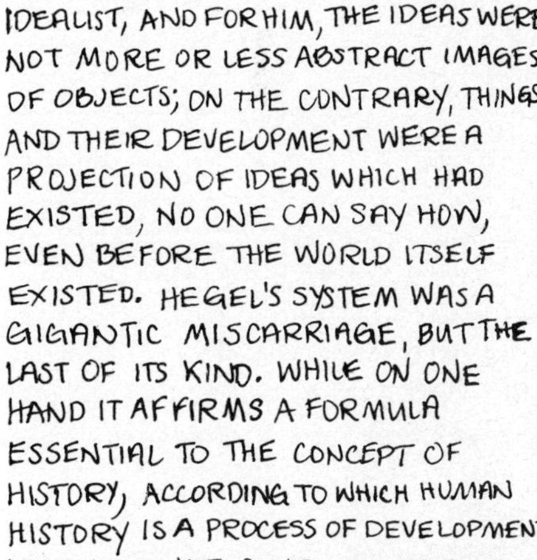

IN ESSENCE:

HEGEL'S PHILOSOPHY CONTAINS LOTS OF VALUABLE IDEAS, SUCH AS HIS THEORY OF ETERNAL MOTION, THE DEVELOPMENT OF UNIVERSAL SPIRIT, AND ESPECIALLY HIS METHOD OF

Dialectics

HE WAS RIGHT WHEN HE SAID THE LAW OF DIALECTICS GOVERNS THE DEVELOPMENT OF SPIRIT (MIND). BUT HE DIDN'T GO FAR ENOUGH AND APPLY IT TO NATURE AND SOCIETY..!

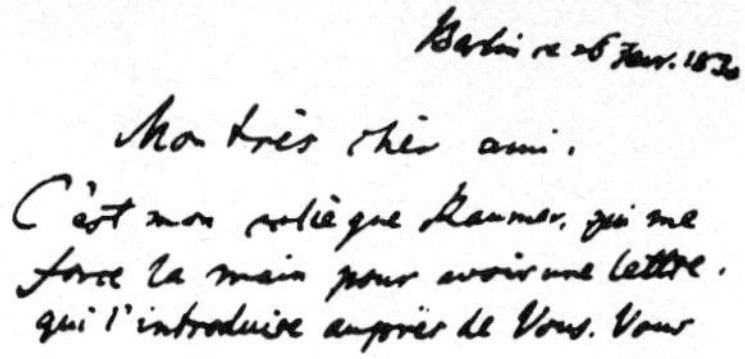

Berlin ce [illegible]

Mon très cher ami.

C'est mon collègue Raumer, qui me force la main pour écrire une lettre, qui l'introduise auprès de Vous. Vous

FROM THE STANDPOINT OF THE DIALECTICAL METHOD, NOTHING IS ETERNAL OR UNCHANGING... BUT IN SPITE OF THIS HEGEL <u>DENIES</u> THE DEVELOPMENT OF NATURE AND SOCIETY,

THIS IS THE MOST SERIOUS CONTRADICTION IN HIS USE OF THE METHOD...

HEGEL (AND I'LL TRY HARD TO BE CLEAR) WAS AN IDEALIST. "THE ESSENCE OF REALITY," HE SAID, "ISN'T MATERIAL, BUT SPIRITUAL (OR MENTAL), AND IS THEREFORE INDEPENDENT AND THUS FREE..."
Great! Now explain that...!
Sure! Hegel says that you can feel free even in chains...
HEGEL'S ADVICE TO ANY WORKER EXPLOITED BY HIS BOSS WOULD BE: DON'T WORRY YOURSELF ABOUT MATERIAL OPPRESSION, BUT ONLY ABOUT THE "SPIRITUAL" KIND. BY OBEYING THE STATE (GOD'S REPRESENTATIVE ON EARTH) YOU WILL FIND HAPPINESS AND FREEDOM (OF THE SPIRIT...)
What the 'ell's he saying?
TODAY, HEGEL'S IDEAS SEEM ABSURD. BUT IN HIS DAY, THEY SOUNDED PRETTY DARING AND THEY WERE ATTACKED JUST BECAUSE THEY WERE (IN THEIR OWN WAY) DIALECTICAL...
Dialectic... yes, but idealist...
THIS LED MARX TO SAY THAT HEGEL'S METHOD WAS "INVERTED", UPSIDE-DOWN, AND IT NEEDED TO BE STOOD ON ITS FEET AGAIN...
...in short, to make it Materialist...
But what does Hegel's theory say about Development?
Well, Let's take it step by step:

HUMAN DEVELOPMENT - SAID HEGEL - HAD GONE THROUGH CONSTANT EVOLUTION, STARTING WITH PRIMITIVE ORIENTAL DESPOTISM, IN WHICH ONLY ONE PERSON WAS FREE (THE TYRANT), AND NEXT THE GRAECO-ROMAN ARISTOCRATIC SYSTEM IN WHICH MANY MORE WERE FREE...

LATER STILL, SLAVERY AND SERFDOM DISAPPEARED, AND EVEN MORE PEOPLE WERE FREE... AFTER THE HOLY ROMAN-GERMAN EMPIRE, FEUDALISM, MONARCHY, THE FRENCH REVOLUTION, AND FINALLY WITH THE PRUSSIAN STATE HUMANITY REACHES (ACCORDING TO HEGEL, ANYWAY)

ABSOLUTE LIBERTY

PRUSSIA HAD AN EMPEROR, AN ARMY, A VERY RICH CHURCH AND SOME BIG LANDOWNERS. THE PEOPLE WORKED FOR THEM, WITHOUT BEING SLAVES MAYBE, BUT OPPRESSED ENOUGH. HEGEL DIDN'T NOTICE THIS OPPRESSION. HE IMAGINED ABSOLUTE LIBERTY EXISTED JUST BECAUSE SLAVERY WAS ABOLISHED...

WHAT WAS REALLY HAPPENING WAS THAT FEUDALISM HAD GRADUALLY GIVEN WAY TO CAPITALISM A MORE MODERN AND SUBTLER FORM OF EXPLOITATION.
... Doctor Hegel didn't take any notice of this...
But MARX did!!
HEGEL WENT ON TALKING ABOUT HUMAN DEVELOPMENT WHILE DENYING IT, BECAUSE HE CLAIMED THE PRUSSIAN STATE HAD BEGUN TO ACHIEVE THIS DEVELOPMENT ALREADY. SO HE TOO SINKS BACK INTO METAPHYSICS...
...Isn't that just like a Government minister!!
HEGEL'S ARGUMENTS REMAIN VALID AND DIALECTICAL, EVEN THOUGH MISTAKENLY APPLIED BY HIM TO REALITY... LET'S SEE, FOR INSTANCE, WHAT HE MAKES OF THE "CONFLICT BETWEEN CONTRARIES"...
"Each thing is a combination of contraries because it is made up of elements which, although linked together, at the same time eliminate one another..."
DON'T HAVE A NERVOUS BREAKDOWN YET,! THERE'S AN EXAMPLE COMING:

SOCIETY, FOR EXAMPLE, IS A COMBINATION OF CONTRARIES (THE RICH AND WELL-OFF *VERSUS* THE POOR AND MISERABLE) HITCHED TOGETHER, YES, BUT OPPOSED...

WITH VERY GOOD RESON, HEGEL SAID THAT WHAT MAKES HUMANITY EVOLVE IS THE STRUGGLE BETWEEN CONTRARIES.
THE TRIUMPH OF ONE OVER THE OTHER PRODUCES CHANGE...

FUNNY, HOW IN HEGEL'S PRUSSIAN STATE THE CONFLICT BETWEEN CONTRARIES WASN'T GOING TO LEAD TO TRANSFORMATION, BUT RATHER AN IMPROVEMENT OF SOCIETY.
THIS SUITED HEGEL, NATURALLY... THAT'S WHY!...

AT THIS POINT, MARX STEPS IN TO PUT HEGEL (AND HIS METHOD) THE RIGHT WAY UP...

IF HEGEL'S DIALECTICAL METHOD INFLUENCED MARX, LUDWIG FEUERBACH (PRONOUNCED "FOY-ER-BACK") TURNED HIM INTO A MATERIALIST.

BUT MARX TOOK OVER FEUERBACH'S THEORY AND CHANGED IT...

FEUERBACH, A DISCIPLE OF THE IDEALIST HEGEL, GAVE UP HEGELIAN IDEALISM TO SWITCH OVER TO MATERIALISM, BUT OF A METAPHYSICAL BRAND, BECAUSE HE SAW NATURE (AND SOCIETY TOO) SUNK IN SLEEP, MOTIVE-AND-MOTIONLESS, WITH NO IMMEDIATE CHANCE FOR CHANGE

THAT IS:

IT WAS UP TO MARX TO RE-SHUFFLE THE DECK: TO AMALGAMATE THE THE BEST OF THIS ONE AND THAT ONE AND COME UP WITH HIS OWN FAMOUS, UNIQUE VARIETY OF

DIALECTICAL MATERIALISM

(Dialectics by G.W.F. Hegel and Materialism by L. Feuerbach)

AS WE'VE NOTED, HEGEL DIDN'T SEE OR DIDN'T WISH TO SEE THE EXPLOITATION OF THE MAJORITY BY A MINORITY OF THE PRIVILEGED RICH. HERE'S THE FIRST QUESTION THE YOUNG MARX ASKED HIMSELF...
Work alienates the worker... But how and why?
(ALIENATION means 'to distract; to seize possession of something, to extort from others what belongs to them'.)
PUBLICITY
UNFREE LABOUR, (IE. WHAT'S DONE FOR A BOSS) MAY EARN THE WORKER A WAGE, BUT AT THE SAME TIME IT "ALIENATES" HIM. IT DEPRIVES HIM OF SOMETHING WHICH GOES INTO THE BOSS'S POCKET.
But is this "something" money or what?
IN HIS FIRST WORK, MARX BEGINS TO INVESTIGATE ALIENATION - OR BETTER, THE DIFFERENT KINDS OF ALIENATION: POLITICAL, RELIGIOUS AND ECONOMIC
This work's called "Economic and Philosophic Manuscripts of 1844"

Marx wonders: where does the product of the workingman's labour end up?

BY HIS LABOUR, A WORKER MAKES SOMETHING (CLOTH, MACHINERY, TYRES, BOOKS, HOUSES...). BUT THIS OBJECT, BY THE FACT OF REMAINING THE BOSS'S PROPERTY, TURNS HEY PRESTO! INTO MERCHANDISE (A *COMMODITY*)...

LABOUR OBVIOUSLY DOESN'T PRODUCE THINGS FOR THE IMMEDIATE BENEFIT OF THE WORKER WHO MAKES THEM. RATHER, IT IS GRIST FOR SOMEONE ELSE'S MILL...

Alienation begins with the worker being squeezed dry...

"...THE ALIENATION OF THE WORKER IS EXPRESSED THUS: THE MORE HE PRODUCES, THE LESS HE CAN CONSUME; THE MORE VALUE HE CREATES, THE LESS VALUE HE HAS... LABOUR PRODUCES FABULOUS THINGS FOR THE RICH, BUT MISERY FOR THE POOR. MACHINES REPLACE LABOUR, AND JOBS DIMINISH, WHILE OTHER WORKERS TURN INTO MACHINES..."

(*Marx: "Manuscripts of 1844"*)

This is how alienation makes its victims...)

ALIENATION NOT ONLY DEGRADES MAN, BUT ALSO DE-PERSONALISES HIM. WHAT CAN YOU EXPECT?

MARX STATES: THE BOSS IMPOSES THE KIND OF WORK, THE METHOD AND THE RHYTHM, BUT HE NEVER BOTHERS IF THE WORKER ENDS UP AS:

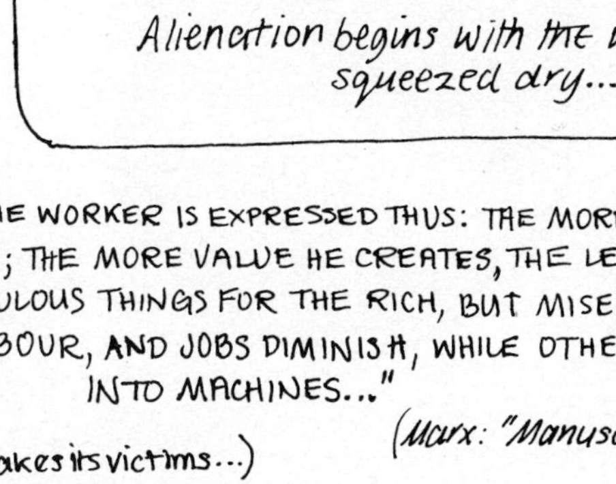

A mere appendage of flesh on a machine of iron...

(*Marx*)

MARX GOES EVEN FURTHER AND AFFIRMS:
THE COMBINED MEANS OF PRODUCTION NOW IN EXISTENCE HAVE BEEN PRODUCED BY THE LABOUR OF PREVIOUS GENERATIONS WHO HAVE THOUGHT, CREATED AND GIVEN THEIR LIVES TO ATTAIN SOMETHING...
So? Who owns the inventions of Galileo, Newton, Leonardo, and thousands of others?
NO ENTRY PRIVATE PROPERTY
IS IT RIGHT THAT ALL OF THIS SHOULD REMAIN IN THE HANDS OF THE FEW? THAT THE INVENTION AND LABOUR OF THOUSANDS OF YEARS SHOULD BE THE EXCLUSIVE PRIVILEGE OF THE WEALTHY FEW?
NO, IT'S NOT RIGHT!
"SOCIAL POTENTIAL HAS BECOME THE PRIVATE POWER OF THE FEW."
MARX ALSO SUBMITS:
THE LABOUR OF THE MANY TRANSFORMS ITSELF INTO THE CAPITAL OF A PRIVILEGED FEW.
PRIVATE OWNERSHIP OF THE MEANS OF PRODUCTION IS THE MAXIMUM FORM OF ALIENATION...
THE ROOTS OF CAPITALISM

AND SO — MARX CONCLUDES — THE DEEPEST ESSENCE OF MAN, HIS CREATIVE ACT, HAS BEEN TRANSFORMED INTO A POSSESSION ...

THE WORKER'S LABOUR BECOMES MERCHANDISE IN THE HANDS OF THE OWNER, DEAD LABOUR, POSSESSION, WEALTH, AND THE GREATER THE CAPITALIST'S PROPERTY BECOMES, THE MORE IMPOVERISHED THE WORKER'S BEING ...

THAT BLESSED "LIBERTY" HEGEL TALKED ABOUT, JUST DOESN'T EXIST. MONEY OBLIGES THOSE WHO HAVEN'T GOT ANY, TO SELL THEMSELVES BODY AND SOUL — THAT IS, TO SELL THEIR LABOUR-POWER (WORKER, PEASANT, INTELLECTUAL)... THIS IS ALIENATION:

EXPLOITATION...

TO POSSESS POSSESSIONS, A MAN WILL "SELL HIMSELF" TO HAVE WHAT ANOTHER HAS. BUT IT NEVER DAWNS ON HIM ~ THAT THE MORE HE GETS, THE LESS HE KEEPS OF HIMSELF...
This guy too aspires to own property. The purpose of his life is to possess more and more and more and...
Bye-bye homo sapiens...
THE COUNTLESS EVILS OF THE WORLD STEM FROM THE "DEFENCE" OF PRIVATE PROPERTY: THE EVILS OF ENVY, WAR, EGOISM, CRIME, INJUSTICE, THE MISERY OF THE MASSES AND LUXURY FOR THE VERY FEW...
I have a hunch that this fellow Marx is going to cause us many a headache...
HOW CAN THIS STATE OF AFFAIRS BE CHANGED?
In no way!! Who's going to tangle with the rich, the powerful, the church...?
MARX SINGLED OUT THE EXISTENCE OF A "NEW" CLASS:
The Proletariat
WHICH CAME TO LIFE WITH THE INDUSTRIAL REVOLUTION WHEN MACHINES BEGAN REPLACING THE CRAFTSMEN OF THE PAST...
a proletarian: someone at the beck and call of the boss's machines...

Marx predicted that this class—the working class—was going to change things...
HOW, AND WITH WHAT POWERS??
UNLIKE THE SMALL-SCALE ARTISANS WHO USED TO OWN THE TOOLS OF THEIR TRADE, THE PROLETARIAT OWNS NOTHING AT ALL—NEITHER THE MEANS, NOR THE END-PRODUCTS...
and still less our labour...
UNLIKE ALL OTHER SOCIAL CLASSES, THE WORKING CLASS POSSESSES ONLY ITS LABOUR POWER, I.E. WHAT IS COMMONLY KNOWN AS THE "WORK FORCE".
GULP!
DIALECTICALLY SPEAKING, THIS IS WHAT SPECIFIES THE STRUGGLE BETWEEN THE CONTRARIES: CAPITAL ON ONE SIDE, LABOUR ON THE OTHER. THEY LIVE TOGETHER, SURE, BUT WITH OPPOSED INTERESTS...

THE OUTLINES OF THE PROBLEM ARE CLEAR: IT ONLY REQUIRES PRACTICAL PROOF, NOT THE WAYWARD LANGUAGE OF PHILOSOPHY WHICH BAFFLES EVERYONE...

Private property has made us so stupid and one-sided that an object is only *ours* when we have it — when it exists for us as capital, or when it is directly possessed, eaten, drunk, worn, inhabited, etc.,—in short, when it is *used* by us . . .

In place of *all* these physical and mental senses there has therefore come the sheer alienation of *all* these senses — the sense of *having*. The human being had to be reduced to this absolute poverty in order that he might yield his inner wealth to the outer world . . .

In order to abolish the *idea* of private property, the *idea* of communism is completely sufficient. It takes *actual* communist action to abolish actual private property. History will come to it; and this movement, which in *theory* we already know to be a self-transcending movement, will constitute *in actual fact* a very severe and protracted process . . .

Marx (extracts from *Manuscripts of 1884*)

THAT'S WHAT MARX RECOGNIZED, AND SO HE SPENT HIS LIFE TRYING TO CREATE A PROLETARIAN PHILOSOPHY...

"JUST AS PHILOSOPHY FINDS ITS MATERIAL WEAPONS IN THE PROLETARIAT, SO THE PROLETARIAT FINDS ITS INTELLECTUAL WEAPONS IN PHILOSOPHY... PHILOSOPHY CAN ONLY BE REALISED BY THE ABOLITION OF THE PROLETARIAT, AND THE PROLETARIAT CAN ONLY BE ABOLISHED BY THE REALISATION OF PHILOSOPHY."

("Critique of Hegel's Philosophy of Right." 1844)

BUT THE PRIMARY NECESSITY WAS TO KNOW WHAT THE PROLETARIAT THOUGHT, TO LIVE AMONG THEM FOR THE PURPOSE OF UNITING THEORY AND PRACTICE... AND THE COUNTRY IN WHICH REVOLUTIONARY PRACTICE HAD MADE MOST PROGRESS WAS

France,

THE BIRTHPLACE IN 1789 OF THE FIRST GREAT REVOLUTION IN HUMAN HISTORY, THE

FRENCH REVOLUTION

AS WE'VE ALREADY SEEN (BUT PROBABLY FORGOTTEN), MARXISM HAS THREE BASIC SOURCES WHICH ARE:

3

GERMAN PHILOSOPHY

ENGLISH POLITICAL ECONOMY

FRENCH SOCIALISM

SINCE WE'VE HAD A LOOK AT THE PHILOSOPHICAL ORIGINS, LET'S GLANCE BRIEFLY AT FRENCH SOCIALISM, STARTING WITH:

GRACCHUS BABEUF

(PLEASED...)

1760
1797

WHEN THE FRENCH REVOLUTION HAD BEEN DEFEATED, AND THE WORTHY JACOBINS WERE IN RETREAT, A SMALL GROUP OF THEM KNOWN AS

THE 'CONSPIRACY OF EQUALS'

HOPED TO CARRY ON THE ARMED STRUGGLE FOR POWER AND THE CREATION OF A SOCIALIST STATE...

WELL, IT'S NOT KNOWN EXACTLY, BUT, FIRST, THE EXPROPRIATION OF WEALTH AND ITS EQUAL REDISTRIBUTION, THE ESTABLISHMENT OF COMMON OWNERSHIP. WORK AND EDUCATION COMPULSORY FOR EVERYONE. BUT THE CONSPIRACY WAS DISCOVERED AND BABEUF CONDEMNED...

THE NEXT ATTEMPTS AT SOCIALISM ALSO OCCUR IN FRANCE, DURING NAPOLEON'S REGIME, BUT THESE ATTEMPTS WERE ONLY THEORETICAL.

THE BIG NAMES HERE ARE

SAINT-SIMON & FOURIER

KNOWN AS "UTOPIAN SOCIALISTS" BECAUSE WHAT THEY WANTED TO ACHIEVE SEEMED "UTOPIAN" OR "IDEALLY PERFECT"...

WHEN SAINT-SIMON DIED, HIS DISCIPLES REALLY STARTED A RELIGION WITH ITS OWN LITURGY, RITES AND THINGS OF THAT SORT. SAINT-SIMON'S THEORY HAD NO SCIENTIFIC BASIS AT ALL AND IT DID NOT ACKNOWLEDGE THE CLASS STRUGGLE...

Fourier

UNLIKE THE ARISTOCRATIC SAINT-SIMON, HE WAS POOR AND SPENT HIS LIFE TRYING TO GET THE RICH TO FINANCE HIS PROJECTS...

Oh! not much! He only wants to build a "communist" system of little communities, in which everything belongs to everyone, with communal homes and consumers' co-operatives. To prevent the rise of wealth in any one sector, the richer would get a smaller part of the share, while the poorer got more, (and thereby balance things out). He actually founded a few such communities (called "Phalanstères"). But he spent his last days in a mad-house...

✻ THERE'S NO DOUBT THAT A FEW OF HIS IDEAS MERIT SOME CONSIDERATION. FOR EXAMPLE, THE ELIMINATION OF COMPETITION AMONG PRODUCERS TO STOP THEM CHURNING OUT USELESS THINGS, DUPLICATES AND LUXURY ITEMS...

SOME OF THE IDEAS OF SAINT-SIMON AND FOURIER WERE PROBABLY TAKEN UP BY MARX (AND LENIN!) IN THEIR OWN, MORE PRACTICAL THEORIES.
BUT THE BIGGEST CONTRIBUTION CAME FROM THREE OTHER FRENCH "SOCIALISTS"...
LOUIS-AUGUSTE BLANQUI (1805 – 1881)
* (sorry! I couldn't find his picture...)
A partisan of class war and armed revolution who spent 33 years of his life in gaol. He first spoke of the Dictatorship of the Prolotariat, even if it was a minority one, and not as Marx argued, in the majority...
BLANQUI, PROUDHON, AND BLANC
Anarchist and syndicalist, but despite this, anti-feminist and an avowed enemy of woman's liberation from domestic slavery. He was the founder of mutual aid societies.
"Property is theft."
PROUDHON 1809-1865
BLANC
1811 1882
Workers' leader, theorist of election-based, legislative socialism, not the violent revolutionary kind.
His most famous saying is: "From each according to his ability, to each according to his need."

MARX CAME INTO CONTACT WITH THEM IN PARIS, OFTEN STRIVING TO SHOW THEM THEIR ERRORS. SOME WERE FISHING IN THE TROUBLED WATER OF ADVENTURISM. OTHERS DIDN'T GRASP MARX'S THEORY AND CALLED IT "UNREALISTIC FOLLY" OR "EXCESSIVELY RADICAL"...

SO MARX HAD SOMETHING NEW TO ADD TO HIS PARIS "MANUSCRIPTS", ANOTHER STUDY WITH THE STRANGE TITLE: THE HOLY FAMILY

Die heilige Familie,

oder

Kritik

der

kritischen Kritik.

Gegen Bruno Bauer & Consorten.

Von

Friedrich Engels und Karl Marx.

IN THIS BOOK, WRITTEN WITH ENGELS, MARX BRINGS TO LIGHT THE CONFLICT OF CONTRARIES WHICH GOES ON WITHIN CAPITALIST SOCIETY, BETWEEN CAPITAL AND LABOUR, THE INEVITABLE REVOLT OF THE WORKING CLASS, AND THE SUBSEQUENT DEFEAT OF THE BOURGEOISIE... IN TWO WORDS: THE CLASS STRUGGLE...

THE AMERICAN TWINS.
"United we stand, Divided we fall."

THIS THESIS WAS OPPOSED THROUGHOUT THE WORLD...

INSTEAD OF CLASS STRUGGLE, CAPITALISM WANTS TO PREACH AN "ALLIANCE" FOR PROGRESS...

BUT THE CLASS STRUGGLE ISN'T JUST MARX'S INVENTION. IT HAS ALWAYS EXISTED (AND MAYBE ALWAYS WILL) EVER SINCE THE WORLD BEGAN
(ALTHOUGH MARX TELLS US IT WON'T ALWAYS EXIST, AS WE SHALL SEE...)

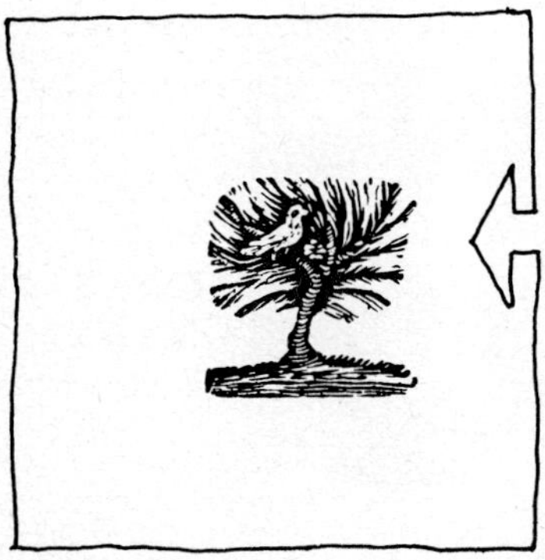

"THE MODERN BOURGEOIS SOCIETY THAT HAS SPROUTED FROM THE RUINS OF FEUDAL SOCIETY, HAS NOT DONE AWAY WITH CLASS ANTAGONISM. IT HAS BUT ESTABLISHED NEW CLASSES, NEW CONDITIONS OF OPPRESSION, NEW FORMS OF STRUGGL
... SOCIETY AS A WHOLE IS MORE AND MORE SPLITTING INTO TWO GREAT HOSTILE CAMPS:

BOURGEOISIE AND PROLETARIAT..."

He never denied what he owed to others—as in this letter to Weydemeyer, dated March 5, 1852:

'And now as to myself, no credit is due to me for discovering the existence of classes in modern society, nor yet the struggle between them. Long before me, bourgeois historians had described the historical development of this class struggle and bourgeois economists the economic anatomy of the classes. What I did that was new was to prove: 1) that the *existence of classes* is only bound up with *particular, historical phases in the development of production;* 2) that the class struggle necessarily leads to the *dictatorship of the proletariat;* 3) that this dictatorship itself only constitutes the transition to the *abolition of all classes* and to *a classless society.*"

WHAT'S IMPORTANT, IS TO GRASP THAT EACH SOCIAL CLASS HAS ITS OWN INTERESTS AND EACH HOLDS VIEWS ABOUT THE GOVERNMENT OF THE STATE CONSISTENT WITH THE DEFENCE OF THOSE INTERESTS...

IT CAN'T, BECAUSE SO LONG AS ANY ONE CLASS LIVES BY EXPLOITING ANOTHER, A STRUGGLE WILL EXIST AGAINST SUCH EXPLOITATION...

IT'S NOT ON BECAUSE THE CAPITALIST SYSTEM HAS ONLY ONE AIM, PROFIT, BASED ON PRIVATE PROPERTY, WHICH IS OBTAINED BY EXPLOITING THE LABOURS OF THE PROLETARIAT...

MARX PROVES WITH GREAT PRECISION THAT UNDER THIS "NEW SYSTEM", (CAPITALISM, THAT IS) THE WORKER IS CONDEMNED NEVER TO ENJOY THE ADVANTAGES WHICH THE SYSTEM RESERVES ONLY FOR THE OWNERS OF THE MEANS OF PRODUCTION...

SO MARX HAD TO SWITCH FROM PHILOSOPHICAL PROBLEMS TO THOSE WHICH PHILOSOPHY USUALLY IGNORES, BUT HE RECKONED THAT IT WAS NECESSARY TO COME TO GRIPS WITH THEM BEFORE HE COULD PROVE HIS THEORIES:

ECONOMIC PROBLEMS

THE PECULIAR MR. MARX WHO NEVER MANAGED TO SOLVE HIS OWN FINANCIAL PROBLEMS (HIS FAMILY OFTEN WENT HUNGRY) WANTS TO RESOLVE THE PROBLEMS OF MILLIONS OF EXPLOITED WORKERS;
IN LONDON, PARIS, ROME, BERLIN, BRUSSELS,

I COULD GO ON ALL DAY...

MARX WAS BY NOW LIVING IN THE DEEPEST POVERTY, WITHOUT SALARY AND WITHOUT CAPITAL...

BUT IT'S EASIER TO UNDERSTAND HIM BY QUOTING FROM A LETTER THAT HE WROTE TO HIS OLD FRIEND ENGELS...

Marx to Engels, Sept. 8, 1852.

"You will have seen from my letters that, as usual when I am right in the shit myself and not merely hearing about it from a distance, I show complete indifference. Anyway, *que faire?* My house is a hospital and the crisis is so disrupting that it requires all my attention . . . The atmosphere is very disturbed: my wife is ill, Jennychen is ill and Lenchen has a kind of nervous fever. I couldn't and can't call the doctor, because I have no money for the medicine. For eight or ten days I have managed to feed the family on bread and potatoes, but it is still doubtful whether I can get hold of any today. . . I have written no articles for Dana because I had not a penny to go and read the newspaper. . . Besides there is the baker, milkman, greengrocer, and old butcher's bills. How can I deal with all this devilish filth? And then finally, during the last eight or ten days I managed to borrow a few shillings and pence which were absolutely necessary if we were to avoid giving up the ghost. . ."

MARX BEGINS: WHAT IS SALARY?

HOW IS IT DEFINED?

If workers were asked: "How much are your wages?" one would reply: "I get a mark a day from my bourgeois," another "I get two marks," and so on. According to the different trades to which they belong, they would mention different sums of money which they receive from their respective bourgeois for a particular period of labour or for the completion of a particular piece of work, e.g. weaving a yard of linen or type-setting a printed sheet. In spite of the variety of their statements, they would all agree on one point: wages are the sum of money paid by the capitalist for a particular period of labour or for a particular output of labour.

The capitalist, it appears, therefore *buys* their labour with money. They *sell* him their labour for money. But this is merely the appearance. In reality what they sell to the capitalist is their labour *power.* The capitalist buys this labour power for a day, a week, a month, etc. And after he has bought it, he uses it by having the workers work for the stipulated time. For the same sum with which the capitalist has bought their labour power, e.g. two marks, he could have bought two pounds of sugar or a definite amount of any other commodity. The two marks, with which he bought two pounds of sugar, are the *price* of the two pounds of sugar. The two marks, with which he bought twelve hours' use of labour power, are the price of twelve hours' labour. Labour power, therefore, is a commodity, neither more nor less than sugar. The former is measured by the clock, the latter by the scales.

(Marx, *Wage-Labour and Capital)*

HAVE YOU UNDERSTOOD?
THE WORKER EXCHANGES HIS COMMODITY (LABOUR-POWER) FOR AN EQUIVALENT WAGE (SO THE BOSS SAYS) TO PURCHASE WHAT HE NEEDS TO SURVIVE: LIGHT, FOOD, ROOF, CLOTHES...

Or rather, just to keep afloat...

BUT IF A WORKER'S PAY WERE CALCULATED ON HIS BASIC NEEDS, IT WOULD HAVE TO BE A VERY GOOD PAY, SO THE BOSSES MIGHT ARGUE...

LET'S CHECK THAT AGAINST THE PROFIT MADE FROM A WORKER'S LABOUR. ENGELS, WHO WAS A 'BOSS' HIMSELF, EXPLAINS HOW...

Let us assume that our worker— a machinist—has to make a part of a machine which he can complete in one day. The raw material—iron and brass in the necessary previously prepared form—costs, twenty marks. The consumption of coal by the steam-engine, the wear and tear of this same engine, of the lathe and other tools which our worker uses, represent for one day, and reckoned by his share of their use, a value of one mark. The wage for one day, according to our assumption, is three marks. This makes twenty-four marks in all for our machine part. But the capitalist calculates that he will obtain, on an average, twenty-seven marks from his customers in return, or three marks more than his outlay.

Whence came the three marks pocketed by the capitalist? According to the assertion of classical economics, commodities are, on the average, sold at their values, that is, at prices corresponding to the amount of necessary labour contained in them. The average price of our machine part—twenty-seven marks—would thus be equal to its value, that is equal to the labour embodied in it. But of these twenty-seven marks, twenty-one marks were values already present before our machinist began work. Twenty marks were contained in the raw materials, one mark in the coal consumed during the work, or in the machines and tools which were used in the process and which were diminished in their efficiency to the value of this sum. There remain six marks which have been added to the value of the raw material. But according to the assumption of our economists themselves, these six marks can only arise from the labour added to the raw material by our worker. His twelve hours' labour has thus created a new value of six marks. The value of his twelve hours labour would, therefore, be equal to six marks. And thereby we would at last have discovered what the "value of labour" is.

(Engels, *Wage-Labour and Capital*)

... IN OTHER WORDS, THE OWNER MAKES IN A DAY WHAT ALL THE WORKERS PUT TOGETHER EARN, AND WITHOUT DIRTYING HIS HANDS, MILORD! ...

IT GOES WITHOUT SAYING — THE WORKER WORKS TO LIVE. WHAT HE EARNS GOES INTO KEEPING HIS FAMILY ALIVE, AND SO HE PASSES THE BEST YEARS OF HIS LIFE DOING WHAT HE DOESN'T LIKE DOING... WHILE THE BOSS GROWS RICHER AND RICHER...

WHILE THE BOSSES RUN TO CONSULT THEIR ECONOMISTS AND IDEOLOGISTS, HOPING TO FIND SOME WAY TO COMBAT HIS THEORIES, MARX CONTINUES: "SALARY IS THE PRICE OF A GIVEN COMMODITY... BUT HOW IS THE PRICE OF A COMMODITY DETERMINED?"...

WHAT DETERMINES THE PRICE OF ANY PRODUCT IS COMPETITION, OR, MORE EXACTLY, THREE KINDS OF COMPETITION:

SELLER VERSUS SELLER

PURCHASER VERSUS PURCHASER

SELLER VERSUS PURCHASER

WHEN SEVERAL VENDORS HAVE THE SAME MERCHANDISE TO SELL, THEY BECOME COMPETITORS WHO MAY RESORT TO CUT-PRICE TACTICS...

WHEN A NUMBER OF PURCHASERS HEAD FOR THE SAME COMMODITY, IT GOES TO ONE WHO'S WILLING TO PAY MORE FOR IT...

COMPETITION BETWEEN SELLER AND BUYER OCCURS WHEN ONE WANTS TO SELL HIGH, AND THE OTHER WANTS TO BUY CHEAP...

That's the law of "supply and demand", kiddo!!
WHEN THERE ARE 100 CARS AND 1000 POSSIBLE BUYERS, THE PRICE OF THE VEHICLE JUMPS UP ACCORDING TO THE WISHES OF THE SELLER... BUT IF THERE ARE 100 CARS AND ONLY 20 BUYERS, IT'S VERY PROBABLE THE PRICE WILL FAVOUR THE BUYER...
But we still don't know what it is that determines prices...
LET'S TALK ABOUT THE PRICE OF PRODUCTION... AN AUTOMOBILE, FOR INSTANCE, JUST OFF THE ASSEMBLY LINE COSTS £1000; ADD TO THIS ALL THE HIDDEN COSTS SUCH AS PUBLICITY, PUBLIC RELATIONS EXCERCISES, THE DISTRIBUTOR'S PERCENTAGE, TAXES, THE PRODUCER'S PROFIT...
Result? The retail price to the public jumps to £2000...

MARX DIDN'T KNOW ABOUT SUCH NOVELTIES AS SALES REPRESENTATIVES, P.R. AND AD. MEN, ALL OF **WHOM** GROSSLY **INFLATE** THE PRICE OF GOODS...

ANYWAY, THE QUESTION HAS BEEN ASKED WHETHER (AND BY HOW MUCH) THE PROFITS OF THE WEALTHY MIGHT BE LIMITED... BY 10%? IS THAT "FAIR AND DECENT"? BUT AT THIS RATE, THE PROBLEM CAN NEVER BE RESOLVED...

SO IT'S THE LABOUR-POWER OF THE WORKER WHICH DAY BY DAY SWELLS THE BOSS'S CAPITAL. THE RICH BECOME EVEN RICHER, WHILE THE POOR CERTAINLY DON'T GET ANY FATTER ON THEIR WAGES (WHICH HARDLY KEEP PACE...)

WHILE THE BOSS, THE CAPITALIST AND THE RICH MAN MAKE A FABULOUS PROFIT FROM THE WORKER'S LABOUR, THE POOR FELLOW DOESN'T MAKE A PENNY EXTRA FOR HIS WORK...

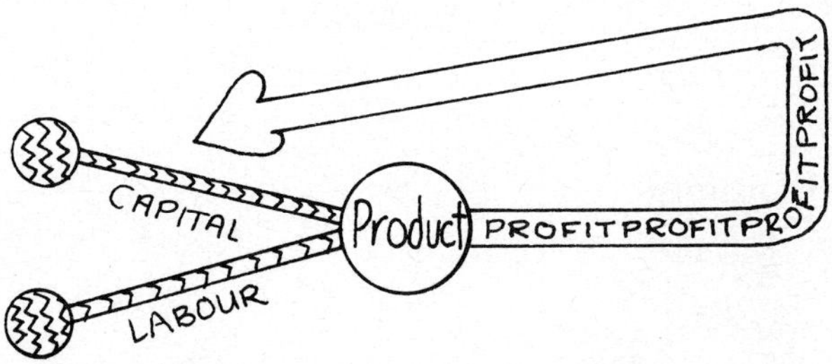

THIS DRAWING ⇧ SHOWS THE PROCESS AT WORK: THE INPUTS OF THE CAPITALIST AND THE WORKER (MONEY FROM ONE AND LABOUR FROM THE OTHER) COMING TOGETHER TO CREATE A PRODUCT.
BUT THE PROFIT FLOWS ONLY IN ONE DIRECTION, NOT BOTH, AS JUSTICE DEMANDS...
SO ONE GROWS FAT WHILE THE OTHER TIGHTENS WHAT'S LEFT OF HIS BELT...

THAT'S HOW OUR CHARLIE CAME TO DISCOVER THE BASIS OF CAPITALISM, THE FAMOUS

SURPLUS VALUE

O.K. LET'S PROCEED. THE BASIC FORMULA OF CAPITALISM IS VERY SIMPLE: BUYING SO AS TO SELL AGAIN FOR PROFIT. THIS INCREASE IN THE VALUE OF THE MONEY EMPLOYED WHICH RESULTS FROM THE TRANSACTION, MARX CALLS SURPLUS VALUE.

MARX REASONED THUS: SURPLUS VALUE CANNOT DERIVE FROM THE MERE EXCHANGE OF GOODS, SINCE THIS IS AN EXCHANGE OF EQUIVALENT THINGS, COMMODITIES ARE SOLD TO BUY OTHER COMMODITIES...

... EVEN LESS DOES SURPLUS VALUE COME FROM INCREASES OF PRICE, SINCE THE RECIPROCAL PROFIT-AND-LOSS BETWEEN BUYERS AND SELLERS TEND TO BALANCE OUT...

TO OBTAIN SURPLUS VALUE (EXTRA PROFIT), THE POSSESSOR OF CASH HAS GOT TO KIND ON THE MARKET SOME OTHER "COMMODITY" WITH THE CURRENT VALUE HAVING THE ONE PECULIAR QUALITY WHICH MAKES IT THE <u>SOURCE OF VALUE</u>...

THE CAPITALIST BUYS THE WORKER'S LABOUR-POWER AS IF IT WAS ANY OTHER KIND OF MERCHANDISE, AND PUTS IT TO WORK EIGHT HOURS A DAY (IN MARX'S TIME, THE WORKING DAY WAS <u>12</u> TO <u>15 HOURS</u>...)

But the worker can make, say, in 6 hours ("necessary" working time) a product which is enough for his livelihood

This surplus product, the boss's extra profit, is surplus value...

In six hours he "produces his salary"...

THANKS TO SURPLUS VALUE, THE BOSS GETS RICHER, WHILE THE WORKER EARNS NOT A PENNY FROM IT. SURE, SOME MONEY IS SUPPOSED TO BE USED TO IMPROVE WORKING CONDITIONS... BUT IT GOES STRAIGHT INTO THE BANK...

To fatten my capital some more...

In the two hours remaining he produces another commodity, a "surplus" product for which his boss doesn't pay him anything...

THIS IS THE TRAP OF PRESENT-DAY CAPITALISM: INCREASING THE WORKER'S PRODUCTIVE OUTPUT AND HIS EFFICIENCY, ALSO INCREASES SURPLUS VALUE...

A RISE IN PRODUCTIVITY IS NOTHING OTHER THAN A WAY TO AUGMENT THE BOSS'S CAPITAL—AND THE POVERTY OF ALL WORKERS...!!

SOMEONE IS SURE TO THINK EVERYTHING COULD BE RESOLVED BY A NICE RAISE IN SALARY

MARX DIDN'T AGREE WITH THIS BECAUSE...

WELL, JUST READ WHAT HE THOUGHT...

Real wages may remain the same, they may even rise, and yet relative wages fall. Let us suppose, for example, that all means of subsistence have gone down in price by two-thirds while wages per day have only fallen by one-third, that is to say, for example, from three marks to two marks. Although the worker can command a greater amount of commodities with these two marks than he previously could with three marks, yet his wages have gone down in relation to the profit of the capitalist. The profit of the capitalist (e.g. the manufacturer) has increased by one mark, that is, for a smaller sum of exchange values which he pays to the worker, the latter must produce a greater amount of exchange values than before. The share of capital relative to the share of labour has risen. The division of social wealth between capital and labour has become still more unequal. With the same capital, the capitalist commands a greater quantity of labour. The power of the capitalist class over the working class has grown, the social position of the worker has deteriorated, has been depressed one stage further below that of the capitalist. *What then is the general law which determines the rise and fall of wages and profits in their reciprocal relation?*
They stand in inverse ratio to each other. Capital's share, profit, rises in the same proportion as labour's share, wages, falls and vice versa. Profit rises to the extent that wages fall; it falls to the extent that wages rise.

(Marx, *Wage-Labour and Capital*)

(WHICH MEANS: THE BOSS NEVER WANTS TO LOSE...)

TAKE THE EXAMPLE OF CONSTRUCTION:
What've I got to do with it?
WELL, BY BUILDING APARTMENT BLOCKS IN WHICH YOU'LL NEVER LIVE AND FROM WHICH YOU'LL NEVER COLLECT RENT, YOU'RE ONLY HELPING THE CLASS WHICH EXPLOITS YOU TO GROW RICHER...
EVEN BY EARNING MORE — INDEED, DOUBLE — THE WORKER'S SITUATION WON'T CHANGE. MARX SAYS IT CLEARLY:
The best salary workers can get, under the most favourable conditions, only reveals in reality the strength and thickness of the golden bars which imprison them, and which only seem to permit them "greater" freedom of action...
* MORE SALARY, MORE PROFIT FOR THE BOSS...
Hang on! That's not from Marx
(You're right! An Austrian Marxist, Ernst Fischer, said it, and he goes on...)
"... THE MISERY OF THE WORKER, ABOVE ALL, CONSISTS OF THE FACT THAT BY WORKING FOR CAPITALISM HE REPRODUCES CAPITAL, AND BY REPRODUCING IT, HE ALSO INCREASES HIS OWN ALIENATION AND MISERY..."
By 'eck! and what do I do then?

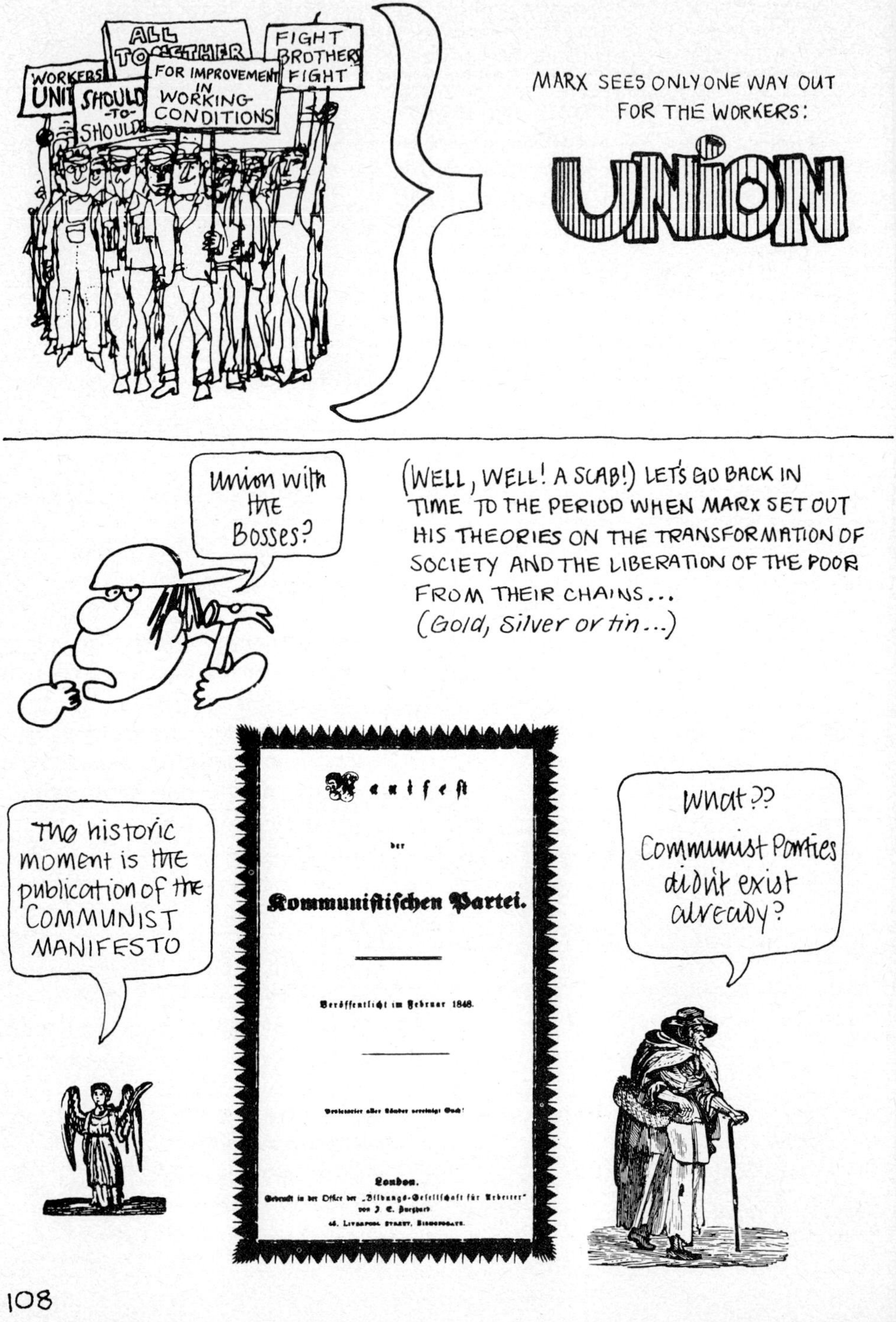
ALL TOGETHER
FIGHT BROTHERS FIGHT
WORKERS UNI
SHOULDER -TO- SHOULDER
FOR IMPROVEMENT IN WORKING CONDITIONS
MARX SEES ONLY ONE WAY OUT FOR THE WORKERS:
UNION
Union with the Bosses?
(WELL, WELL! A SCAB!) LET'S GO BACK IN TIME TO THE PERIOD WHEN MARX SET OUT HIS THEORIES ON THE TRANSFORMATION OF SOCIETY AND THE LIBERATION OF THE POOR FROM THEIR CHAINS...
(Gold, Silver or tin...)
The historic moment is the publication of the COMMUNIST MANIFESTO
Manifest der Kommunistischen Partei.
Veröffentlicht im Februar 1848.
London.
What?? Communist Parties didn't exist already?

The *Manifesto* was published as the platform of the Communist League, a workingmen's association, first exclusively German, later on international, and, under the political conditions of the Continent before 1848, unavoidably a secret society. At a Congress of the League, held in London in November 1847, Marx and Engels were commissioned to prepare for publication a complete theoretical and practical party program. Drawn up in German, in January 1848, the manuscript was sent to the printer in London a few weeks before the French revolution of February 24th. A French translation was brought out in Paris, shortly before the insurrection of June 1848. The first English translation, by Miss Helen Macfarlane, appeared in the *Red Republican*, London, 1850. A Danish and a Polish edition had also been published. . . The first Russian translation, made by Bakunin, was published at Herzen's *Kolokol* office in Geneva, about 1863. . .
However much the state of things may have altered during the last 25 years, the general principles laid down in this *Manifesto* are, on the whole, as correct today as ever.

(Engels, 1888 preface to the *Communist Manifesto)*

BACK IN THOSE DAYS (1846-47), THERE WAS A GROUP MADE UP OF GERMAN WORKERS, ARTISANS AND INTELLECTUALS OF THE AVANT-GARDE (I.E. OF ADVANCED IDEAS) CALLING ITSELF THE "LEAGUE OF THE JUST", WHICH MET TO TALK POLITICS AND KEEP IN TOUCH WITH THE "JUST" MEN IN OTHER COUNTRIES...

THE "JUST" WERE HALF ANARCHIST AND PREACHED A PRETTY STRANGE FORM OF SOCIALISM: DESTRUCTION OF THE MEANS OF PRODUCTION (BLOWING UP FACTORIES, PREFERABLY WITH THE BOSSES IN THEM) AND A RETURN TO AGRICULTURE AND ARTISAN CRAFTSMANSHIP... IN FEBRUARY 1847, MARX AND ENGELS WERE INVITED TO JOIN THE LEAGE TO HELP TO REORGANISE IT...

TOUGH-MINDED GERMANS, AS THEY ALWAYS REMAINED, MARX AND ENGELS ORGANISED A LONDON CONGRESS IN 1847 WHICH BROUGHT IN DELEGATES FROM EVERY CORNER OF EUROPE.
AND HERE, ENGELS PROPOSED HIS **"CREDOS"** OF THE COMMUNIST LEAGUE WHICH SERVED AS THE PLATFORM OF THE "COMMUNIST MANIFESTO"....
(ALSO KNOWN AS THE "PRINCIPLES OF COMMUNISM", 1847)

Question 1: *What is communism?*

Answer: Communism is the doctrine of the prerequisites for the emancipation of the proletariat.

Question 2: *What is the proletariat?*

Answer: The proletariat is that class of society whose means of livelihood entirely depend on the sale of its labor and not on the profit derived from capital; whose weal and woe, whose life and death, whose whole existence depend on the demand for labor, hence on the alternation of good times and bad, on the vagaries of unbridled competition. The proletariat, or class of proletarians, is, in a word, the working class of the 19th century.

Question 3: *Proletarians, then, have not always existed?*

Answer: No. Poor folk and working classes have always existed. The working classes have also for the most part been poor. But such poor, such workers as are living under conditions indicated above, hence proletarians, have not always existed, any more than free and unbridled competition has always existed.

Question 4: *How did the proletariat originate?*

Answer: The proletariat originated in the industrial revolution which took place in England during the second half of the 18th century and which has repeated itself since then in all the civilized countries of the world. This industrial revolution took place owing to the invention of the steam engine, of various spinning machines, of the power loom, and of a great number of other mechanical instruments. These machines were expensive and, consequently, could only be installed by persons who had plenty of capital to lay out. Their introduction completely altered the existing method of production and displaced the existing workers. This was due to the fact that machinery could produce cheaper and better commodities than could the handicraftsmen with their imperfect spinning wheels and hand looms. Thus, these machines handed over industry entirely to the big capitalists and rendered the little property the workers possessed (tools, hand looms, etc.) entirely worthless. Soon the capitalists got all in their hands and nothing remained for the workers.

Question 7: *In what way does the proletarian differ from the slave?*

Answer: The slave is sold once and for all. The proletarian must sell himself by the hour or by the day. Each individual slave, being the direct property of a master, has his existence assured, be that existence ever so wretched, if only because of the interest of the slave owner. Each individual proletarian, the property as it were of the whole bourgeois *class,* whose labor is sold only when it is needed by the owning class, has no security of life. Existence is merely guaranteed to the working *class* as a whole. The slave is excluded from competition; the proletarian is beset by competition and is a prey to all its fluctuations. The slave is counted an object and not a member of civil society; the proletarian is recognized as a person, as a member of civil society. The slave may therefore be able to secure better conditions of life than can the proletarian, but the proletarian belongs to a higher stage of development of society than the slave. The slave frees himself by rupturing, of all relations of private ownership, only one, the relation of slavery and by this act becomes himself a proletarian; the proletarian can only achieve emancipation by abolishing private property in its entirety.

Question 16: *Will it be possible to bring about the abolition of private property by peaceful methods?*

Answer: This is greatly to be desired, and communists would be the last persons in the world to stand in the way of a peaceful solution. Communists know only too well the futility and, indeed, the harmfulness of conspiratorial methods. They know only too well that revolutions are not made deliberately and arbitrarily, but that everywhere and at all times revolutions have been the necessary outcome of circumstances quite independent of the will or the guidance of particular parties and whole classes. But they also perceive that the development of the proletariat in nearly all civilized countries is violently suppressed, and that in this way opponents of communism are working full force to promote a revolution. Should the oppressed proletariat at long last thus be driven into a revolution, then we communists will rally to the cause of the workers and be just as prompt to act as we are now to speak.

Question 17: *Will it be possible to abolish private property all at once?*

Answer: No. This would be just as impossible as to multiply all at once the existing forces of production to the degree necessary for the inauguration of the community. The proletarian revolution, which in all probability is coming, will for this reason, only be able to transform present society gradually. Private property will be abolished only when the means of production have become available in sufficient quantities.

The *Manifesto* is a direct appeal to all workers—*Workers of the World, unite*! It defends the Communist position that the emancipation of the working class itself must be the act of the working class itself. Its lucid, powerful arguments are still potent today. It moves us to take a definite position against the structure of a society in which the unjust division of wealth contradicts basic decency.

Modern industry has established the world market, for which the discovery of America paved the way. This market has given an immense development to commerce, to navigation, to communication by land. This development has, in its turn, reacted on the extension of industry; and in proportion as industry, commerce, navigation, railways extended, in the same proportion the bourgeoisie developed, increased its capital, and pushed into the background every class handed down from the Middle Ages.

We see, therefore, how the modern bourgeoisie is itself the product of a long course of development, of a series of revolutions in the modes of production and of exchange.
The bourgeoisie, wherever it has got the upper hand, has put an end to all feudal, patriarchal, idyllic relations. It has pitilessly torn asunder the motley feudal ties that bound man to his "natural superiors", and has left remaining no other nexus between man and man than naked self-interest, than callous "cash payment". It has drowned the most heavenly ecstasies of religious fervour, of chivalrous enthusiasm, of philistine sentimentalism, in the icy water of egotistical calculation. It has resolved personal worth into exchange value, and in place of the numberless indefeasible chartered freedoms, has set up that single, unconscionable freedom—Free Trade. In one word, for exploitation, veiled by religious and political illusions, it has substituted naked, shameless, direct, brutal exploitation.
The bourgeoisie has born away from the family its sentimental veil, and has reduced the family relation to a mere money relation.

The bourgeoisie, during its rule of scarce one hundred years, has created more massive and more colossal productive forces than have all preceding generations together. Subjection of Nature's forces to man, machinery, application of chemistry to industry and agriculture, steam-navigation, railways, electric telegraphs, clearing of whole continents for cultivation, canalisation of rivers, whole populations conjured out of the ground—what earlier century had even a presentiment that such productive forces slumbered in the lap of social labour?

Owing to the extensive use of machinery and to division of labour, the work of the proletarians has lost all individual character, and, consequently, all charm for the workman. He becomes an appendage of the machine, and it is only the most simple, most monotonous, and most easily acquired knack, that is required of him. Hence, the cost of production of a workman is restricted, almost entirely, to the means of subsistence that he requires for his maintenance, and for the propagation of his race. But the price of a commodity, and therefore also of labour, is equal to its cost of production. In proportion, therefore, as the repulsiveness of the work increases, the wage decreases.

But Big Mama Television wasn't around yet to stupefy us all the more before going to bed...

Modern industry has converted the little workshop of the patriarchal master into the great factory of the industrial capitalist. Masses of labourers, crowded into the factory, are organised like soldiers. As privates of the industrial army they are placed under the command of a perfect hierarchy of officers and sergeants. Not only are they slaves of the bourgeois class, and of the bourgeois State; they are daily and hourly enslaved by the machine, by the over-looker, and, above all, by the individual bourgeois manufacturer himself. The more openly this depotism proclaims gain to be its end and aim, the more petty, the more hateful and the more embittered it is.

The less the skill and exertion of strength implied in manual labour, in other words, the more modern industry becomes developed, the more is the labour of men superseded by that of women. Differences of age and sex have no longer any distinctive social validity for the working class. All are instruments of labour, more or less expensive to use, according to their age and sex.

No sooner is the exploitation of the labourer by the manufacturer, so far, at an end, that he receives his wages in cash, than he is set upon by the other portions of the bourgeoisie, the landlord, the shopkeeper, the pawnbroker, etc.

But with the development of industry the proletariat not only increases in number; it becomes concentrated in greater masses, its strength grows, and it feels that strength more. The various interests and conditions of life within the ranks of the proletariat are more and more equalised, in proportion as machinery obliterates all distinctions of labour, and nearly everywhere reduces wages to the same low level. The growing competition among the bourgeois, and the resulting commercial crises, make the wages of the workers ever more fluctuating. The unceasing improvement of machinery, ever more rapidly developing, makes their livelihood more and more precarious; the collisions between individual workmen and individual bourgeois take more and more the character of collisions between two classes. Thereupon the workers begin to form combinations (Trades' Unions) against the bourgeois; they club together in order to keep up the rate of wages; they found permanent associations in order to make provision beforehand for these occasional revolts. Here and there the contest breaks out into riots.

... And here's how Marx formulates the class struggle ...

Now and then the workers are victorious, but only for a time. The real fruit of their battles lies, not in the immediate result, but in the ever-expanding union of the workers. This union is helped on by the improved means of communication that are created by modern industry and that place the workers of different localities in contact with one another. It was just this contact that was needed to centralise the numerous local struggles, all of the same character, into one national struggle between classes. But every class struggle is a political struggle. And that union, to attain which the burghers of the Middle Ages, with their miserable highways, required centuries, the modern proletarians, thanks to railways, achieve in a few years.
This organisation of the proletarians into a class, and consequently into a political party, is continually being upset again by the competition between the workers themselves. But it ever rises up again, stronger, firmer, mightier. It compels legislative recognition of particular interests of the workers, by taking advantage of the divisions among the bourgeoisie itself. Thus the ten-hours' bill in England was carried.

Of all the classes that stand face to face with the bourgeoisie today, the proletariat alone is a really revolutionary class. The other classes decay and finally disappear in the face of modern industry; the proletariat is its special and essential product.
The lower middle class, the small manufacturer, the shopkeeper, the artisan, the peasant, all these fight against the bourgeoisie, to save from extinction their existence as fractions of the middle class. They are therefore not revolutionary, but conservative. Nay more, they are reactionary, for they try to roll back the wheel of history. If by chance they are revolutionary, they are so only in view of their impending transfer into the proletariat, they thus defend not their present, but their future interests, they desert their own standpoint to place themselves at that of the proletariat.
The "dangerous class", the social scum, that passively rotting mass thrown off by the lowest layers of old society, may, here and there, be swept into the movement by a proletarian revolution; its conditions of life, however, prepare it far more for the part of a bribed tool of reactionary intrigue.

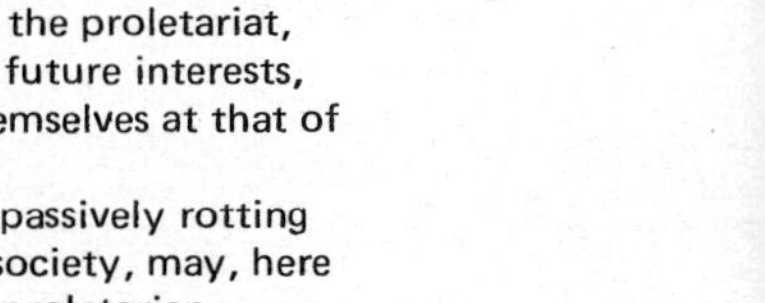

All property relations in the past have continually been subject to historical change consequent upon the change in historical conditions.
The French Revolution, for example, abolished feudal property in favour of bourgeois property.
The distinguishing feature of Communism is not the abolition of property generally, but the abolition bourgeois property. But modern bourgeois private property is the final and most complete expression of the system of producing and appropriating products, that is based on class antagonisms, on the exploitation of the many by the few.
In this sense, the theory of the Communists may be summed up in the single sentence: Abolition of private property.
We Communists have been reproached with the desire of abolishing the right of personally acquiring property as the fruit of a man's own labour, which property is alleged to be the ground work of all personal freedom, activity and independence.
Hard-won, self-acquired, self-earned property! Do you mean the property of the petty artisan and of the small peasant, a form of property that preceded the bourgeois form? There is no need to abolish that; the development of industry has to a great extent already destroyed it, and is still destroying it daily.
Or do you mean modern bourgeois private property?
But does wage labour create any property for the labourer? Not a bit. It creates capital, i.e. that kind of property which exploits wage labour, and which cannot increase except upon condition of begetting a new supply of wage labour for fresh exploitation.
Property, in its present form, is based on the antagonism of capital and wage labour. Let us examine both sides of this antagonism.

You are horrified at our intending to do away with private property. But in your existing society, private property is already done away with for nine-tenths of the population; its existence for the few is solely due to its non-existence in the hands of those nine-tenths. You reproach us, therefore, with intending to do away with a form of property, the necessary condition for whose existence is, the non-existence of any property for the immense majority of society.

BUT THE WORLD WOULD GO TO RACK AND RUIN
OR SO THEY SAY...

In one word, you reproach us with intending to do away with your property. Precisely so; that is just what we intend.
From the moment when labour can no longer be converted into capital, money, or rent, into a social power capable of being monopolised, i.e. from the moment when individual property can no longer be transformed into Bourgeois property, into capital, from that moment, you say, individuality vanishes.
You must, therefore, confess that by "individual" you mean no other person than the bourgeois, than the middle-class owner of property. This person must, indeed, be swept out of the way, and made impossible.

It has been objected that upon the abolition of private property all work will cease, and universal laziness will overtake us. According to this, bourgeois society ought long ago to have gone to the dogs through sheer idleness; for those of its members who work, acquire nothing, and those who acquire anything, do not work. The whole of this objection is but another expression of the tautology: that there can no longer be any wage-labour when there is no longer any capital.

The bourgeois sees in his wife a mere instrument of production. He hears that the instruments of production are to be exploited in common, and, naturally, can come to no other conclusion than that the lot of being common to all will likewise fall to the woman.
He has not even a suspicion that the real point aimed at is to do away with the status of women as mere instruments of production.
For the rest, nothing is more ridiculous than the virtuous indignation of our bourgeois at the community of women which, they pretend, is to be openly and officially established by the Communists. The Communists have no need to introduce community of women; it has existed almost from time immemorial.

Our bourgeois, not content with having the wives and daughters of their proletarians at their disposal, not to speak of common prostitutes, take the greatest pleasure in seducing each other's wives.
Bourgeois marriage is in reality a system of wives in common and thus, at the most, what the Communists might possibly be reproached with, is that they desire to introduce, in substitution for a hypocritically concealed, an openly legalised community of women. For the rest, it is self-evident that the abolition of the present system of production must bring with it the abolition of the community of women springing from that system, i.e. of prostitution both public and private.

This situation changed with the patriarchal family and even more with the monogamous individual family. The administration of the household lost its public character. It was no longer the concern of society. It became *private service*. The wife became the first domestic servant, pushed out of participation in social production. Only modern large-scale industry again threw open to her — and only to the proletarian woman at that — the avenue to social production; but in such a way that, when she fulfils her duties in the private service of her family, she remains excluded from public production and cannot earn anything; and when she wishes to take part in public industry and earn her living independently, she is not in a position to fulfil her family duties. What applies to the woman in the factory applies to her in all professions, right up to medicine and law. The modern individual family is based on the open or disguised domestic enslavement of the woman; and modern society is a mass composed solely of individual families as its molecules. Today, in the great majority of cases, the man has to be the earner, the breadwinner of the family, at least among the propertied classes, and this gives him a dominating position which requires no special legal privileges. In the family, he is the bourgeois; the wife represents the proletariat.

We have seen above, that the first step in the revolution by the working class, is to raise the proletariat to the position of ruling class, to win the battle of democracy.
The proletariat will use its political supremacy to wrest, by degrees, all capital from the bourgeoisie, to centralise all instruments of production in the hands of the State. i.e. of the proletariat organised as the ruling class; and to increase the total of productive forces as rapidly as possible.
Of course, in the beginning, this cannot be effected except by means of despotic inroads on the rights of property, and on the conditions of bourgeois production; by means of measures, therefore, which appear economically insufficient and untenable, but which, in the course of the movement, outstrip themselves, necessitate further inroads upon the old social order, and are unavoidable as a means of entirely revolutionising the mode of production.
These measures will of course be different in different countries.

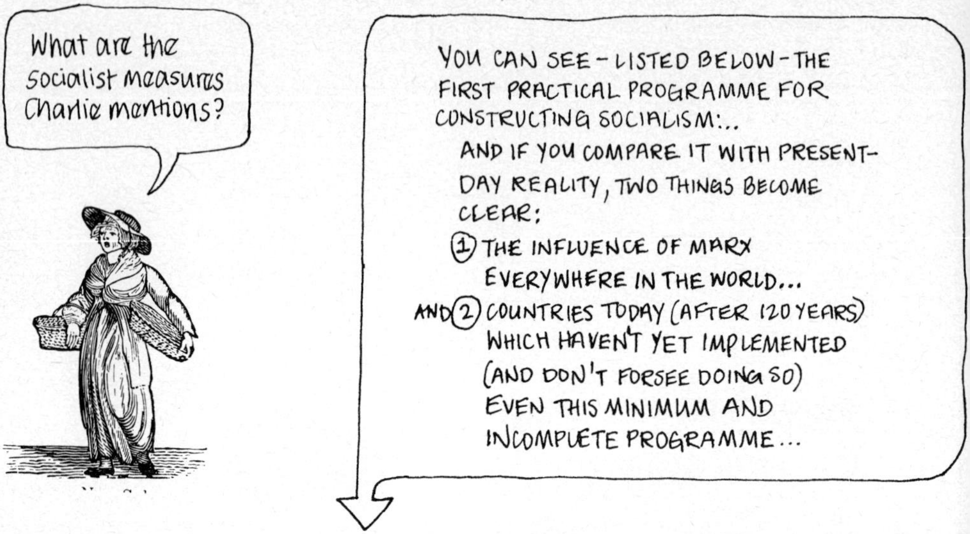

Nevertheless in the most advanced countries, the following will be pretty generally applicable:

1. Abolition of property in land and application of all rents of land to public purposes.
2. A heavy progressive or graduated income tax.
3. Abolition of all right of inheritance.
4. Confiscation of the property of all emigrants and rebels.
5. Centralisation of credit in the hands of the State, by means of a national bank with State capital and an exclusive monopoly.
6. Centralisation of means of communication and transport in the hands of the State.
7. Extension of factories and instruments of production owned by the State; the bringing into cultivation of waste-lands, and the improvement of the soil generally in accordance with a common plan.
8. Equal liability of all to labour. Establishment of industrial armies, especially for agriculture.
9. Combination of agriculture with manufacturing industries; gradual abolition of the distinction between town and country, by a more equable distribution of the population over the country.
10. Free education for all children in public schools. Abolition of children's factory labour in its present form. Combination of education with industrial production, &c., &c.

HERR KARL MARX (ALIAS THE "TOUGH GUY") FORCEFULLY DEMONSTRATES THAT CAPITALISM IS INCAPABLE OF RESOLVING THE PROBLEMS OF HUMANITY. SO LONG AS THE SYSTEM GOES ON DEVELOPING, EVERYTHING WILL GO FROM BAD TO WORSE... A DECADENT EMPIRE SPREADING LIKE A PLAGUE EVERYWHERE...
Is that -gulp- North American Imperialism..?
WHY'S THAT?
What went wrong with the bourgeoisie who'd started off so well?
Why has it produced gangster representatives like Hitler, Trujillo, the Brazilian apes, Truman Franco, Pinochet, Nixon and the rest...?
MARX COULDN'T MAKE IT ANY PLAINER. ALL SYSTEMS WHICH CARRY THE DESTRUCTIVE SEEDS OF CLASS WAR WILL EVENTUALLY DISAPPEAR... BUT BEFORE GOING UNDER, THEY DEFEND THEMSELVES TO THE DEATH LIKE SAVAGE, WOUNDED BEASTS, UNTIL THE UP-AND-COMING SYSTEM ADMINISTERS THE COUP-DE-GRÂCE...
THE INTERNAL CRISES OF THE YANKEE EMPIRE, THE STRUGGLE FOR SOCIALISM IN VIETNAM, CUBA, CHILE, AFRICA, THE SPLITS INSIDE THE CHURCH, EVERY LIBERATION MOVEMENT... ARE ALL SIGNS OF CAPITALISM'S LAST STRUGGLES TO AVOID BEING WIPED OFF THE FACE OF THE EARTH...
Vietnam and Chile prove glaringly who the real enemy of humanity is...
Yeah! Greed!!
$卐$卐

CAPITALISM HAS PROVEN ITSELF UNABLE TO SOLVE THE PROBLEMS OF THE PEOPLE LIVING UNDER IT (NOT TO MENTION PROBLEMS IN GENERAL OF HUMANITY)... AND IT'S WELL ON THE ROAD TO FINAL CRISIS AND EVENTUAL COLLAPSE.

THE PURPOSE OF MARX'S THEORY OF

HISTORICAL MATERIALISM

IS TO SHOW US THAT HISTORY IS MADE BY MAN, NOT BY "DESTINY" OR THE SO CALLED "HAND OF GOD"...

HUMANITY – THOUGHT MARX – DID NOT REQUIRE 'OUTSIDE' HELP TO INVENT ITS TOOLS. NO ANGEL APPEARED FROM HEAVEN TO TEACH MAN HOW TO CONSTRUCT PLOUGHS AND WHEELS...

EACH GENERATION COMES ALONG TO CREATE, AND GRADUALLY PERFECT NEW TOOLS – BY WORKING AND NOT THANKS TO THE HOLY SPIRIT! (EVEN IF NOT ALL THE GREAT INVENTORS WERE ATHEISTS...)

BUT TOOLS CANNOT WORK ALL BY THEMSELVES.

PEOPLE HAVE TO SWEAT TO KEEP THEM OPERATING...

THESE INSTRUMENTS OF PRODUCTION, AND THE MEN WHO PRODUCE THINGS WITH THEM, ARE WHAT MARX CALLS...

BUT NOTHING IS PRODUCED IN ISOLATION. HUMAN LABOUR ALWAYS HAS A SOCIAL CHARACTER. SOCIETY WAS FORMED BY MEN AS A HELP, AS A PROTECTION AGAINST WILD ANIMALS, TO GET BETTER RESULTS FROM WORK...

EXACTLY.
BECAUSE THIS IS WHAT EVENTUALLY HAPPENED. THE OWNERS JOINED FORCES TO SQUEEZE PRODUCTIVITY OUT OF THE NON-OWNERS (I.E. THOSE WHO HAD NOTHING BUT THEIR LABOUR-POWER...)

(AND THAT'S HOW, AS WE'VE SEEN, THE LEVELS OF SOCIAL CLASS AROSE, AND HOW THE PRECISE KINDS OF RELATIONS BETWEEN THEM WERE SET UP.
ONE EXPLOITERS,
THE OTHER EXPLOITED...)

THESE RELATIONS, WHICH PEOPLE ESTABLISH (LIKE 'EM OR NOT) DURING THE PROCESS OF PRODUCTION, MARX CALLS:

The relations of production

THE COMBINATION OF "PRODUCTIVE FORCES" (OR UNITS OF PRODUCTION) AND THE RELATIONS OF PRODUCTION, MARX DEFINES BY THE CONCEPT OF

MODE OF PRODUCTION

HISTORY ISN'T JUST THE LIFE AND ADVENTURES OF NOBLES, KINGS, PRIESTS AND SUCH, BUT IT REVEALS THE SUCCESSIVE STAGES OF THE DIFFERENT MODES OF PRODUCTION BY WHICH MANKIND GAINED POWER OVER NATURE.

MARX DISTINGUISHES 5 SYSTEMS OR MODES THUS:

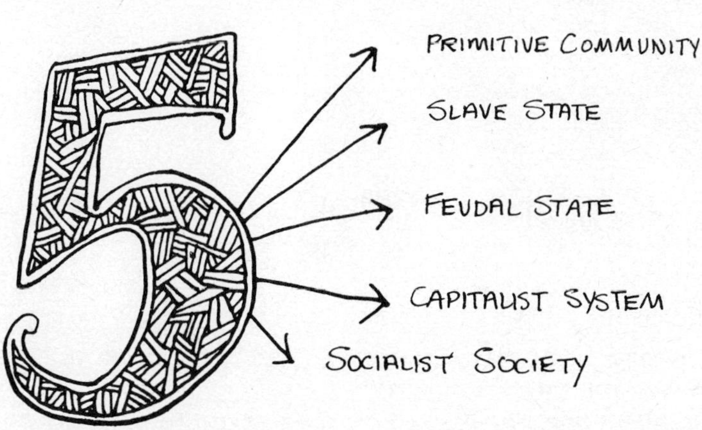

THE SYSTEM WE'LL NOW TRY TO EXPLAIN IS...

Feudalism (hoping even my wife'll understand it!)

FEUDALISM COMES FROM THE LATIN WORD, "FEUDUM", THE NAME GIVEN TO THE LANDS WHICH THE KING DIVIDED UP AMONG HIS NOBLES IN EXCHANGE FOR THEIR SUPPORT... (A "FEUDUM" = A "FEE")

THOSE WHO ACTUALLY LIVED ON THE LAND HAD SOME CLAIM TO THEIR BIT OF EARTH. BUT THEIR LABOUR BELONGED TO THE FEUDAL OVER-LORD TO WHOM THEY PAID TAXES AND WHO USED THEM WHENEVER HE WENT TO WAR... WHEN I SAY "KING" BY THE WAY, YOU CAN JUST AS WELL READ "POPE", BECAUSE THE CHURCH OF CHRIST WAS ALSO A FEUDAL SYSTEM LIKE ANY OTHER (AND PROBABLY WORSE...)

WITHIN FEUDALISM, THE SOCIAL CLASSES SEEN FROM TOP TO BOTTOM WERE:

AS TIME WENT ON, THE MERCHANTS AND GUILD ARTISANS GREW IN NUMBERS AND POWER. THEY BEGAN TO SHRUG OFF THE BURDENSOME YOKE IMPOSED ON THEM BY THE NOBLES AND CLERGY. THE FIRST INTELLECTUALS AWOKE, BRINGING NEW IDEAS INTO DAYLIGHT. A NEW CLASS IS BORN, THE

BOURGEOISIE

COMMERCE THUS BEGAN TO CHANGE THE FORM OF PRODUCTION.
THE BOURGEOISIE NEEDED BIGGER (AND FREE) MARKETS TO SHIFT THE MERCHANDISE PRODUCED IN THEIR WORKSHOPS. THEIR APPETITE FOR PROFITS RAN SMACK AGAINST THE LIMITS OF THE FEUDAL MODE OF PRODUCTION...
AND THESE RESTRAINTS PROVOKED A SERIES OF BOURGEOIS

REVOLUTIONS

AGAINST KINGS AND CHURCH, LEADING TO THE BIRTH OF A NEW "SYSTEM OF PRODUCTION":

CAPITALISM

THE FRENCH REVOLUTION WAS PRIMARILY A LIBERATION MOVEMENT.

'LIBERATION' FROM WHAT?

FROM THE POWER OF THE MONARCH AND THE CLERGY.

FOR WHAT?

TO DEFEND PRIVATE PROPERTY AND FREE ENTERPRISE.

FOR WHOSE BENEFIT?

THE BOURGEOISIE, I.E. THE RICH WHO WANTED THE LIBERTY TO MAKE MORE MONEY AND THE LIBERTY OF THE SERFS SO AS TO BUY THEIR LABOUR FREELY.

THE FRENCH REVOLUTION WAS A GENERAL CLASS STRUGGLE, A TOUGH PITCHED BATTLE IN WHICH EVERYONE TOOK SIDES AGAINST THE COMMON ENEMY:
THE NOBILITY AND THE CLERGY.

ONCE DEFEATED, THEIR POWER WENT TO THE ASCENDING CLASS – THE BOURGEOISIE.
THE PEASANTRY GOT SOMETHING OUT OF IT: OWNERSHIP OF THEIR LANDS. BUT THE SERF-LABOURERS GOT NOTHING AT ALL...

THE BOURGEOIS REVOLUTION (OR THE FRENCH: SAME DIFFERENCE) WAS FOLLOWED BY ANOTHER REVOLUTION – THE INDUSTRIAL. HUMANITY INVENTED MACHINES WHICH TOOK THE PLACE OF MANUAL CRAFTS. THIS COMPLETELY REVOLUTIONIZED THE MODE OF PRODUCTION...

THE APPEARANCE ON THE SCENE OF MACHINE-PRODUCED GOODS BRINGS WITH IT A COUPLE OF NEW SOCIAL CLASSES: CAPITALISTS, OR OWNERS OF THE MACHINES, AND WORKERS, OR THE OPERATORS TIED TO THESE INFERNAL MACHINES. WITH MACHINERY COMES A NEW MODE OF PRODUCTION WHICH MARX CALLS

CAPITALISM

NOW THE WORKER ISN'T THE SLAVE OF A FEUDAL LORD. HE'S A "FREE CITIZEN" (I.E. FREE TO SELL HIMSELF TO THE "HIGHEST" BIDDER...)

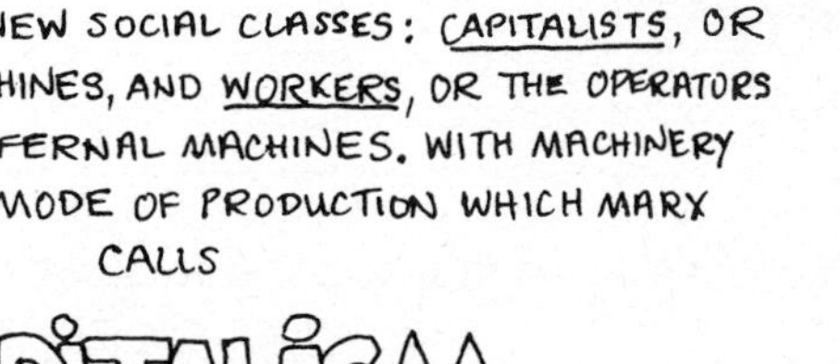

MARX'S THEORY OF CLASS STRUGGLE– INEVITABLE AND HISTORICAL– REALLY HIT CAPITALISM BELOW THE BELT. SOONER OR LATER, SAYS MARX, CAPITALISM IS GOING TO HAVE TO RETREAT BEFORE A NEWER AND FAIRER SYSTEM...

MARX SHOWS US HOW THE LAWS OF HISTORICAL DEVELOPMENT DETERMINE THE INEVITABLE SEQUENCE OF MODES OF PRODUCTION: FROM PRIMITIVE TO SLAVERY, FROM FEUDALISM ON TO CAPITALISM... WHICH LED (AND STILL LEADS) MANY TO ASK THEMSELVES:

MARX Replies:

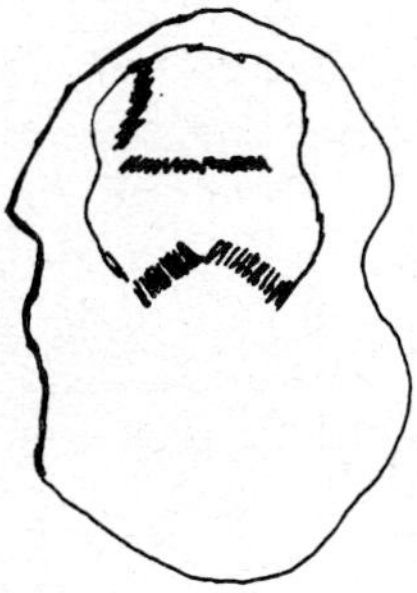

BECAUSE MEN MAKE HISTORY, NOT THE OTHER WAY ROUND...

HISTORY DOESN'T DO ANYTHING. IT DOESN'T PROMOTE ANY STRUGGLE.

CAPITAL WILL ATTEMPT TO RESIST ITS OWN DOWNFALL. WHAT WILL LEAD TO ITS DESTRUCTION ARE CAPITALISM'S INTERNAL CONTRADICTIONS; BUT ONLY BECAUSE OF AN ADVERSARY DEVELOPING INDEPENDENTLY OF CAPITALISM'S WILL, I.E. THE PROLETARIAT...

MARX KNOWS PERFECTLY WELL THAT THE RICH WILL NEVER FREELY SURRENDER THEIR WEALTH AND PRIVILEGES...

HOW?

WELL, IF ANYONE REALLY WANTED TO KNOW (INCLUDING THIS FAT RUSSIAN FAUNTLEROY), MARX WILLINGLY EXPLAINED THE RECIPE FOR TRANSFORMING CAPITALIST SOCIETY INTO A SOCIALIST ONE: EXPROPRIATING THE PRIVATE MEANS OF PRODUCTION, REPLACING THE GOVERNMENT AND STATE ADMINISTRATION...
I.E. SEIZING POWER...

BUT HOW CAN THE WORKERS SEIZE POWER??

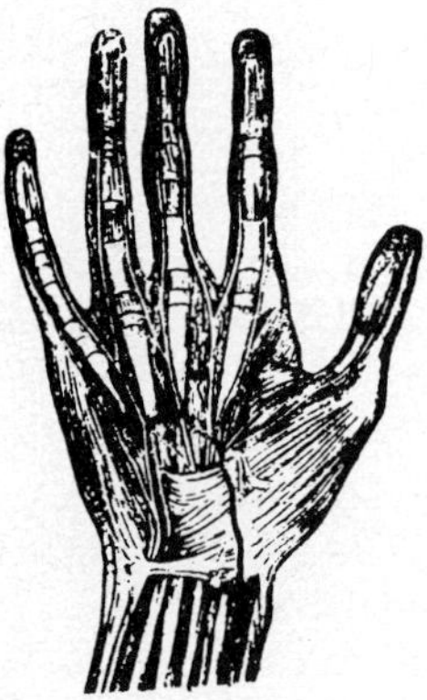

A HAND IS MADE UP OF 5 FINGERS, BUT A FIST IS THE SAME 5 FINGERS UNITED...

(NOT FOR NOTHING, THE FIST IS THE SYMBOL OF THE WORKERS' STRUGGLE...)

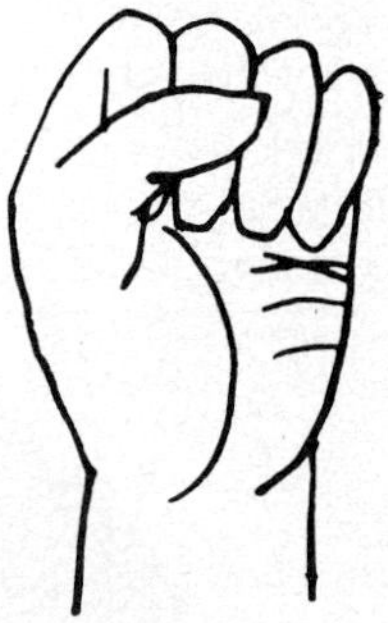

AND SO?

MARX MAKES THE POINT CRYSTAL CLEAR— AS IN THIS ILLUSTRATION:

"IN ITS STRUGGLE AGAINST THE UNITED POWER OF THE RULING CLASS, ONLY THE WORKING CLASS — AS AN ORGANISED CLASS — CAN ACTIVATE A PARTY OF ITS OWN TO OPPOSE ALL OTHER OLD, REACTIONARY PARTIES..."

THE FIRST STEP MUST BE TO CONVINCE THE WORKER THAT ONLY UNITY WILL GIVE HIM THE MEANS TO CHANGE HIS EXISTENCE. HE MUST BECOME AWARE OF HIS POWER, OF THE REASONS WHY HE LIVES BADLY, AND THAT CAPITALISM WILL NEVER SOLVE HIS PROBLEMS. HE MUST REALISE WHAT SOCIALISM CAN OFFER HIM...

...IN A WORD (HE'S GOT TO BE)

POLITICIZED

ONLY A POLITICIZED WORKING CLASS CAN MOVE TO THE NEXT STAGE: THE ORGANIZED STRUGGLE TO SAFEGUARD ITS RIGHTS...

EVEN IN MARX'S DAY, SOME ALREADY BELIEVED THAT UNION CAMPAIGNS ONLY SERVED TO OBTAIN HIGHER WAGES AND BETTER LIVING CONDITIONS... BUT, SAYS MARX, THIS IS THE WRONG WAY TO UNDERSTAND UNIONS...

THE PRINCIPLE AIM OF ANY LABOUR UNION MUST BE CHANGE WHICH ANTICIPATES SOCIALISM ... OR ELSE IT JUST WASTES ITS TIME, AS AMERICAN UNIONS DO, STRUGGLING ALONG ON BENDED KNEE FOR CAPITALISM'S SAKE ...

NOW COMES THE INTERESTING QUESTION, WHICH MANY READERS HAVE PROBABLY ASKED THEMSELVES: PEACEFUL ROAD OR ARMED STRUGGLE? WHICH?

SOONER OR LATER – MARX SAID – THE CONFRONTATION HAS GOT TO TURN DEADLY, AND THE WORKING CLASS WILL ARRIVE AT REVOLUTION.
A WORKERS' PARTY MAY HELP THE PROLETARIAT TO SCREW CONCESSIONS FROM THE CAPITALISTS, BUT EVEN THAT WON'T CHANGE THE BASIC EXPLOITIVE CONDITIONS (MORE OR LESS EXPLOITED, MAYBE, BUT NEVER COMPLETELY FREE ...)

THE STRUGGLE OF INDUSTRIAL AND AGRARIAN WORKERS WITHIN THE FRAME OF UNIONS, PARTIES AND EVEN PARLIAMENT, IS ONLY A WAY TO PREPARE, TO ORGANIZE, TO GAIN THE STRENGTH FOR THE DECISIVE BLOW...

"... in times when the class struggle nears the decisive hour, the process of dissolution going on within the ruling class, in fact within the whole range of old society, assumes such a violent, glaring character..."

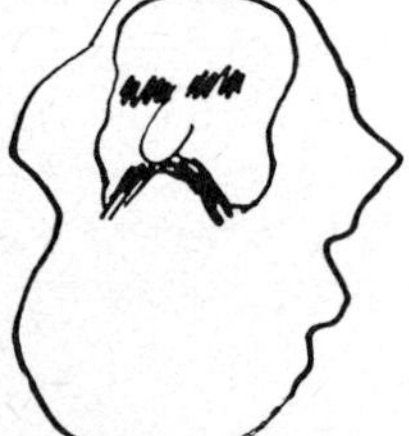

"... that a small section of the ruling class cuts itself adrift, and joins the revolutionary class... just as, at an earlier period, a section of the nobility went over to the bourgeoisie..." (Manifesto)

THIS "SMALL SECTION" CUTTING ITSELF ADRIFT FROM THE BOURGEOISIE INCLUDES INTELLECTUALS, LIKE MARX AND ENGELS, LENIN, MAO, HO CHI MINH, FIDEL CASTRO, CHE, AND LOTS OF OTHERS WHO WOULD HAVE DONE NOTHING <u>ALONE</u>... LIKE THE STUDENTS WHO WON'T CHANGE ANYTHING UNLESS THEY JOIN FORCES WITH THE WORKERS AND PEASANTS...

(amen!!)

MARX NEVER IMAGINED A WORKING CLASS MOVEMENT SEPARATE FROM SOCIALIST THEORY. A SOCIALIST PARTY WITHOUT MASS SUPPORT IS A PHANTOM, A BODY WITHOUT A HEAD, OR VICE VERSA, LIKE THE LEFTIST PARTIES WHICH HAVE LOST TOUCH WITH THE REAL PROBLEMS OF WORKERS AND PEASANTS...

MARX'S THEORY HAD TO WAIT 24 YEARS AFTER HIS DEATH BEFORE BEING PUT INTO PRACTICE, AND IN A COUNTRY WHERE IT SEEMED IMPOSSIBLE. IN RUSSIA, 1917, THANKS TO THE VISION AND STEADFAST STRUGGLE OF A "BOURGEOIS" MARXIST CALLED

Lenin

..."THE TEACHING OF MARX IS ALL-POWERFUL BECAUSE IT IS TRUE. IT IS COMPLETE AND HARMONIOUS, PROVIDING MEN WITH A CONSISTENT VIEW OF THE UNIVERSE, WHICH CANNOT BE RECONCILED WITH ANY SUPERSTITION, ANY REACTION, ANY DEFENCE OF BOURGEOIS OPPRESSION. IT IS THE LAWFUL SUCCESSOR OF THE BEST THAT HAS BEEN CREATED BY HUMANITY IN THE 19th CENTURY — GERMAN PHILOSOPHY, ENGLISH POLITICAL ECONOMY AND FRENCH SOCIALISM."

("The 3 Sources and 3 Component Parts of Marxism" 1913 V.19)

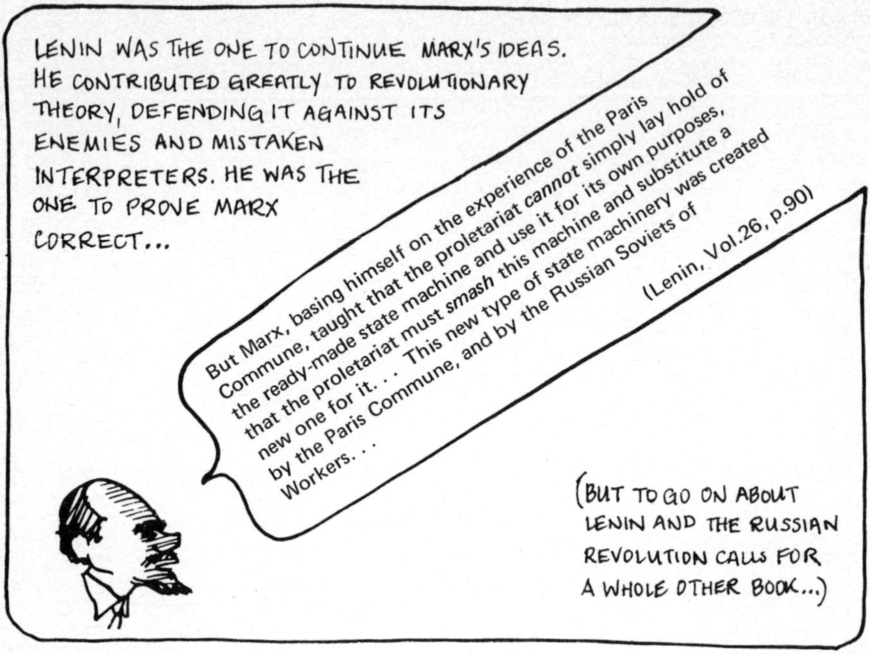

...I THINK THIS IS THE RIGHT PLACE TO WRITE

The End...

(...well, not entirely...)

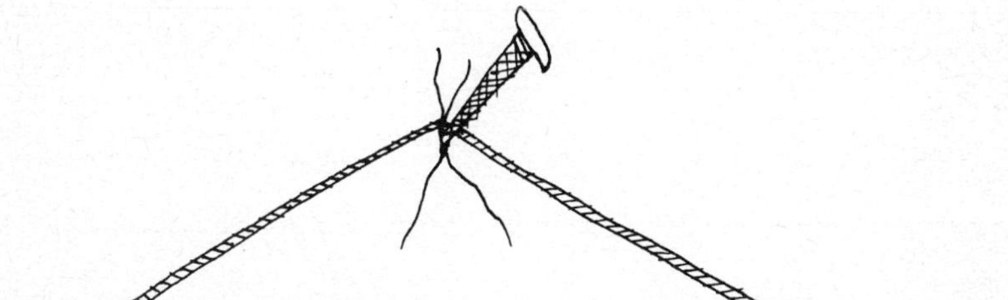

* You're not obliged to read this now! Declare a holiday and start again — later on! And I hope it will be clearer than the preceding pages...

AGNOSTICISM / (from the Greek, *agnostos* = unknown). Philosophical doctrine which maintains that human reason is limited and the true nature of things inaccessible to man. This doctrine holds that the world we observe and deal with is not an objective reality, but rather a product of the activity of our reason and sense organs. Agnosticism is disproved by experience and practice, now that science has cleared the way to the knowledge of things. There remains one difference: between what is already known and what is not yet known.
Agnostic philosophers include Hume, Kant, Comte, Spencer, Mach etc.

ANALYSIS and **SYNTHESIS** / 1) analysis (in Greek, 'decomposition'), dis-integration of an object or phenomenon into its simple component parts. 2) synthesis (in Greek, 'composition'), recombination of the parts of an object or phenomenon as a whole.
Metaphysics opposes analysis to synthesis. Dialectical materialism, instead, maintains the unity of these two procedures. "Without analysis there is no synthesis" (Engels). For example, when analysing the human body, anatomists study its organs separately; but to grasp the complete, deep significance and function of every organ, analysis is not enough. It is necessary to consider the organism as a whole: indeed, studying its parts, but as a synthesis.

ANIMISM / (from the Latin, *anima*: soul). The spiritualization of natural phenomena. The belief that behind every natural object there hides an invisible or 'mental' spirit-force. "This tendency to personification had as a consequence the creation of the gods." (Engels). Primitive animism was the basis of religion and later idealist thought.

ANTAGONISM / (from the Greek, *agon* = contest). An irreconcilable contradiction which is resolved by violence. As the contradiction between the bourgeoisie and the working class is thus resolved by socialist revolution. Contradictions between the working class and peasantry have no antagonistic character.

ATHEISM / (from the Greek, 'without god') The scientific negation of religion. Atheism was born in ancient Greece with the materialist philosophers, Democritus and Epicurus, who denied the supernatural and stated that the world is nothing other than matter composed of atoms.

ANTI-DUHRING / The abbreviated title of a work by Engels: "The Scientific Revolution of Eugene Duhring", a classic of Marxist literature. The work was aimed against the German philosopher, Duhring, who wished to refute Marxism by recourse to metaphysics. The ANTI-DUHRING is a masterly synthesis of Marx's forty years of struggle and study.

ATOM / The idea of the atom was first introduced to science by Democritus and Epicurus, more than 2,000 years ago. The physicist, Newton, and the philosophers, Holbach and Gassendi, worked on this theory.

BASE (or INFRA) and **SUPERSTRUCTURE/** The mode of production, i.e. the forces and relations of production which constitute the economic base - the foundation of society. Once the base (or infrastructure) is modified then the superstructure (including the political system, religion, philosophy, morality, art, science etc.) must also modify itself, at a more or less rapid rhythm. (see also ECONOMIC BASE)

CAPITAL / or 'Das Kapital', the principal work by Karl Marx. A detailed analysis of the laws governing the economic development of capitalism — but also an immense historical and philosophical treatise. In this work, the theory of historical materialism is fundamentally developed.

CATEGORIES / Notions which express the essential relations and laws of the real world. In dialectical materialism, these categories are: matter, motion, space, time, necessity, causality, quantity, substance, form, content, etc. In Historical Materialism, they are: the social-economic structure, forces of production, infra-and super-structure, ideology, etc.
These categories represent a generalization of the processes and phenomena of nature, independent of the consciousness of man.

CAUSALITY / One of the forms of general interdependence of phenomena in the objective world. In essence, cause and effect

"are only moments of interdependence and universal relation, of the connection of events; they are, above all, present in the chain of the development of matter." (Lenin) There can be no phenomena (events) without causes. All natural phenomena have natural and material causes. Cause and effect stand in reciprocal relation to each other. Between them exists an internal relation regulated by laws.
Thus in the socialist system, the development of technology becomes a *cause* of the increasing well-being (*effect*) of workers.

CLASS STRUGGLE (see also **SOCIAL CLASSES**) / Struggle between exploited and exploiters. Demonstration that class interests are irreconcilable. The forms of class struggle are diverse: economic, political, ideological, theoretical. But all such kinds are subordinate to the *political* struggle. With the establishment of the dictatorship of the proletariat, class struggle does not cease but takes on new forms.

COMMUNISM / The doctrine of Marx and Engels founded on the basis of the materialist conception of history. Communism is the stage following after socialism and when social classes cease to exist. Communism does not yet exist in any country. The Soviet Union, China and other socialist countries are still in the phase of socialism where class struggle has still not terminated.

CONDITIONS OF THE MATERIAL LIFE OF SOCIETY / The elements determining the conditions of material life in society are: 1) geographical situation and natural resources; 2) population density; 3) the mode of production by which it creates the material goods necessary to its existence.
The fundamental force which determines development of a society, and also its passage from one kind of social system to another, is material production — the development of the "productive power of the society".

DARWIN, CHARLES (1809-1882) / Celebrated English thinker, founder of the theory of evolution. "Darwin put an end to the belief that the animal and vegetable species bear no relation to one another, except by chance, and that they were created by God, and hence immutable." (Lenin)

DETERMINISM and **INDETERMINISM** / *Determinism*: doctrine concerning the necessary relationship between events and phenomena and their accidental conditioning. For example, the anarchy of the capitalist mode of production fatally *determines* economic crisis; the development of class struggle inevitably *determines* a social revolution.
Idealists oppose to determinism, *indeterminism* — maintaining that the natural course of events in reality are not subject to laws but to independent, arbitrary chance.

DIALECTIC / (from the Greek, 'debate' and 'converse') According to early Greek philosophers, the art of knowing truth by uncovering the contradictions in the reasonings of one's adversary. Later, dialectics (also sometimes in the form, 'dialectic') came to be transformed into a theory of development and universal relations. Dialectics considers all phenomena as being in movement, in process of perpetual change. It views the development of nature itself as a result of the struggle between contradictions within nature. Dialectics became a science when Marx and Engels liberated it from Hegelian idealism. It is a doctrine of development — a science of the universal laws governing the development of nature, human society and thought.

DICTATORSHIP OF THE PROLETARIAT / The period of transition from socialism to communism, during which the material conditions are created for socialist construction, the suppression of classes and the passage to a classless and stateless society.

DOGMA, DOGMATISM / Dogma is undemonstrated affirmation, accepted with blind faith. This is why Marx and Engels always said: "Our doctrine is not a dogma, but a guide to action." Unfortunately, dogmatic Marxists often ignore this crucial aspect of Marxism, and thereby rob it of its revolutionary, creative power.

DUALISM / (from the Latin, 'two') A philosophical tendency opposed to 'monism' (from the Greek, *monos* = one, unity). Dualism places not one but two different substances at the origin of existence. Thus DESCARTES sees man as being composed of two distinct substances: one, material — the body, the other spiritual — the soul. Marxism places matter-in-movement at the origin of all natural phenomena as primary cause. Consciousness is a secondary cause produced by matter.

ECLECTICISM / Mere mechanical link-ups of various currents, concepts and theories, without any pre-established principle. Eclectic thinkers attempt to reconcile materialism and idealism.

ECONOMIC BASE / The mode of production at the basis of any social system. The economic base (or infra-structure) determines the totality of the social superstructure: the state, political institutions, ideas and theories, etc. "The structures of every society can change rapidly only by revolutionizing the economic base." (Marx)

ECONOMIC STRUCTURE / Ordering of society into classes: the *relations* of production which correspond to the specific level determined by the development of the *material* forces of production.

EMPIRIO-CRITICISM / Reactionary, idealist current of philosophy which arose in Germany and Austria during the second half of the 19th century. Its initiators were Avenarius and Mach. They affirmed that "elements of the world" i.e. "elements of experience" stood at the basis of all phenomena. Each thing is a "combination of elements". By the term 'elements', they meant the fact that sensation is at the basis of phenomena; but in such a way as to identify 'element' with sense-impression.

EPICURUS / (342-270 B.C.) Greek materialist philosopher, teacher and follower of Democritus.

EVOLUTION and **REVOLUTION** / Quantitative changes, of an unperceived, slow and interrupted kind come about through evolution. Qualitative changes, on the contrary, happen all at once, by leaps, in a revolutionary manner. Development implies both, necessarily. Evolution prepares the way for revolution. But opportunism replaces revolutionary struggle by reform.

EXISTENCE Philosophic term designating *subjective* reality, in matter.

EXISTENCE and **SOCIAL CONSCIOUSNESS** / From the viewpoint of dialectical materialism, existence is primary while consciousness, as a simple reflection of matter, of nature, of human thought, is secondary. Social existence — i.e. the mode of producing material goods, objects, food, clothing etc. — is the primary element which determines social consciousness and the spiritual, intellectual life of society (its culture). Marx extended materialism into the areas of social phenomena by discovering that social existence and the mode of production determine social consciousness.

EXPERIMENT / By experiment is currently understood the 'practical experience' of the procedures verifying knowledge by direct observation of phenomena — either in the laboratory or in objective reality.
Philosophy explains *experiment* either in materialist or idealist form. For dialectical materialism, experience presupposes the presence of an objective, material world which exists independently of human consciousness. But for idealism, experience does not involve material objects or even phenomena: rather, it is concerned with our past impressions. It can therefore consider religious 'sentiment' alone as *experimental* proof enough of the existence of God.

FATALISM / (from the Latin, 'fate') Idealist notion which holds that historical development is pre-determined by some unknown force, by 'destiny'. Fatalism denies the *creative* function of people, history and political struggle, and considers humanity a plaything in the hands of God or fate, unable to influence things through ACTION.

FETISHISM / To deify or 'fetishize' objects means to give them occult, supernatural forces foreign to human nature. In primitive times, the fetish was an object of awe; later becoming a good or bad luck charm. In capitalism, the fetishism of money, property and commodities is the magic of capitalist ownership.

FEUERBACH, LUDWIG (1804-72) / One of the major German materialists who proclaimed and defended atheism and influenced the founders of Marxism. Feuerbach, however, remains idealist in his concept of social phenomena. Neglecting the material basis of society, he distinguished the successive stages of human development according to the different forms of religious consciousness. Feuerbach did not grasp the importance of practical revolutionary action, or the dialectical interaction between man and nature and the transformation of humanity in the process of production.

FIDE-ISM / (from the Latin, *fides*: 'faith') Doctrine (especially in Latin countries) which replaces understanding by faith and stresses the determinating role it plays. Lenin sees idealist philosophy as a "more or less weakened or diluted fide-ism"; so to speak, a clericalism. (see IDEALISM)

FORCES OF PRODUCTION / Instruments or tools with which material goods are produced; also *persons* who use these productive tools and manufacture material goods, thanks to experience and work-training. Productive forces (machines, tools, raw materials etc.) and human labour-power must be present as the indispensable elements of work. Social life depends upon productive forces which it can command and the modes of production employed. Hence the importance of the *social planning* of these forces, which will only bear fruit with socialism.

FORM and **CONTENT** / In nature, society or thought, everything has its content and form. Agrarian reform, for instance, may be the content; but its form may vary according to the modes of application.

FORMAL LOGIC / Theory concerning the laws of human thought which separates nature from the enquiry into those laws. Formal logic does not preoccupy itself with material truth (i.e. the faithful reflection and conception of natural phenomena), but with 'formal' truth. Hence its name. Herein lies the basis of metaphysical method. Dialectics (i.e. natural logic) is the contrary of formal logic since it considers that the content of thought, the principles and laws of logic, must correspond to materiality, nature and its regulative laws. Formal logic affirms that all objects and concepts are equal to themselves (i.e. the concept of *formal* identity: that A=A). Dialectical materialism shows that every object *is* and *is not* self-identical because it is caught up in a process of development.

FREEDOM and **NECESSITY** / Metaphysicians often contrast freedom to necessity. Some affirm that will is absolutely free, i.e. unconditioned. Others hold that free will does not exist, but only absolute necessity. Either freedom or necessity . . . From the Marxist viewpoint, these positions are un-scientific, because freedom does not merely consist of imaginary independence vis-a-vis the laws of nature, but of knowledge of these laws and the possibility of applying them positively in practical action. "Freedom", Engels says, "consists of a domination over self and external nature; a domination based on the knowledge of the necessities of nature. Consequently, freedom is *conscious necessity*. Without an understanding of necessity, real liberty is unattainable."

HEGEL, GEORG WILHELM FRIEDRICH / (1770-1831) German philosopher, idealist dialectician. Nature, according to Hegel, does not develop across time, but varies eternally only in space. The most valuable part of idealist Hegelian philosophy is the dialectical method it employs — that ideas develop from dialectical contradictions; that transformations from quantity to quality have their origin in this development; that truth is concrete; that the developmental process of human society is realized by its submission to laws and not by chance or under the pressure of outsized personalities. Yet, Hegel was pusillanimous and inconsistent: he bowed before the Prussian feudal monarchy, and minimized the extremes of his dialectical positions out of fear and self-interest. "My dialectical method," Marx said, "is not only distinct from Hegelian method at bottom, but is absolutely opposed to it." For Hegel, thought creates reality. The opposite for Marx — ideas are nothing more than matter absorbed and transformed by human thought.

HUMANISM / Cultural current, developed from the 14th to the 16th centuries.

Conception of social reality proper to the then new-born bourgeoisie which struggled to liberate human personality and science from bondage to religious feudalism. Petrarch, Boccaccio, Erasmus, Machiavelli etc., were some representatives of bourgeois humanism. Humanism cannot survive under a capitalist regime because it is opposed to the exploitation of man by man, the very essence of capitalism. Only the real liberation of humanity can bring about genuine humanism.

HUME, DAVID / (1711-1776) English bourgeois philosopher, historian and economist. As an agnostic, he reckoned insoluble the problem of the existence or non-existence of objective reality. He affirmed that we cannot know what things are in themselves and whether they exist or not. Denying the material basis of things and causality, Hume concluded that what alone exists is a flux of psychological perception in human consciousness, and that science leads only to the simple description of this current, with little possibility either of understanding or of conceiving its laws.

IDEALISM / Philosophy which considers reality as an incarnation of a 'universal Idea' or of a 'consciousness'. Idealism is closely linked with religion and leads more or less openly to the idea of God.

IDEOLOGY / Combination of ideas, assumptions, notions of determined concepts, representations. Politics, science, morality, art and religion are *forms* of ideology. All ideologies are reflections of social existence. In class-based society, ideology expresses and defends the interests of the classes in struggle. In bourgeois society, struggle develops between bourgeois and socialist ideologies. There is no intermediate term, since, as Lenin affirms, humanity has not elaborated a 'third' ideology.

INDUCTION (and **DEDUCTION**) / *Induction:* method of reasoning which consists of passing from the particular to the general, from facts to generalizations. *Deduction:* method which consists of passing from the general to the particular, from generalized propositions to particular conclusions.

INSTRUMENTS (or **TOOLS) OF PRO – RODUCTION** / Principle elements of productive forces (e.g. machinery) employed by humanity to act upon nature and transform it into material goods. Marx says that economic epochs differ from each other not so much in what they produce but *how* they do so. How labour produces. The means of production are not simply measures of human labour-power but also the indication of the *relations* by means of which work takes place.

KANT, IMMANUEL / (1724-1804) Founder of classical German idealism. He attempted to reconcile materialism and idealism. "When Kant admits that a certain 'thing-in-itself', outside us, must correspond to our representation of it, then he is a materialist. When he declares it impossible to know this 'thing-in-itself', he becomes an idealist." (Lenin) As Kant himself declares, the central problem of his theory of knowledge is to define the limits of the laws of reason, while still retaining a place for God beyond such limits. In his doctrine of ethics, Kant believes it 'necessary' to recognize the existence of God and the soul's immortality, so as to maintain a basis for morality.

MARXISM-LENINISM / Theory of the proletarian liberation movement. Theory and practice of the dictatorship of the proletariat. Theory of the construction of communist society.

MATTER / (or **MATERIAL**) By its nature, the world is material. The variety of phenomena in nature corresponds to the distinct forms of *matter in motion.* Lenin wrote that matter is a philosophical category to designate objective reality which presents itself to humanity through human perception. Matter is copied, 'photographed' or reflected through human sensations while retaining an existence proper to itself and independent of them.

MATERIALISM / One of the two main tendencies in philosophy which gives a specific reply to the fundamental problem of the relation between thought and existence. Materialism recognizes matter as the primary element, and consciousness (or thought) secondary. It relies on science — particularly the physical sciences. Dialectical materialism recuperates the entire materialist tradition preceding it and re-elaborates everything of value in it. (see below)

MATERIALISM (DIALECTICAL) / Philosophical doctrine formulated by Marx and Engels, so called because of its *dialectical* manner of confronting, studying and understanding natural phenomena; and *materialist* by its manner of interpreting phenomena and drawing up its theory. Dialectical materialism is the only scientific interpretation of the world; and it is opposed to idealism which offers an interpretation based on religion.

MATERIALISM (HISTORICAL) / Marxist doctrine of the development of human society. Historical materialism sees in the development of material goods necessary to human existence the primary force which determines all social life (and which conditions the transition from one kind of social order to another).

The growth of human power over nature finds its expression in the development of the productive forces of society. The transmutation of economic-social forces throughout history (primitive communal, slave, feudal and capital states) is, above all, a change from certain kinds of productive *modes* and *relations* towards other more progressive ones. Such change is the necessary effect, the cause of which are the laws to which social productive forces everywhere submit.

Discovery of the real basis of life and social development (material production) allows one to see for the first time the importance of the creative spirit of the masses. Great men were not the ones *alone* to make history, but the workers, the real prime movers of the production process, those who accomplished the material tasks necessary for social subsistence.

MATERIALISM (MECHANISTIC) / Early form of materialism which sought to explain all natural phenomena by mechanical laws. It considers motion not as *change* in general but as the mechanical displacement of bodies in space due to external influences — the mere collision of two entities. Mechanistic materialism denies the spontaneous movement of bodies, their qualitative change, the development by leaps, the passage from inferior to superior.

METAPHYSICS / (from the Greek, *ta meta ta physika*: those works of Aristotle after his 'Physics') Metaphysical method affirms that things and their mental reflections (i.e. concepts) are essentially discrete, unchanging, petrified, given once for all, and can thus be investigated separately, independently one from the other. Metaphysics posits in principle that nature is at rest, immobile, unchanging and unmoving. It considers the process of development uniquely on a quantitative and not qualitative level. Politically, the stance is one that denies class struggle and tries to show that the transition from capitalism to socialism can be realized without violent rupture, by peaceful fusion of capitalism with socialism.

METHODOLOGY / Doctrine of method: combination of procedures, techniques of enquiry applicable to all sciences.

MONISM / (from the Greek, *monos*: one) Philosophical doctrine which, contrary to dualism, recognizes as the cause of all existence only a single principle or origin. Materialists, for instance, consider *matter* as the unique cause of all phenomena; and the idealist-monist, spirit or god or mind.

MORALITY, MORALS / Norms of social life, human behaviour, one of the forms of social consciousness. Materialists hold that morality changes with each change of social order. There exists a morality typical of the slave state; another in the feudal state, the bourgeois, and the communist. The ruling class imposes 'its' morality and puts it into practice in accord with its historical class interests.

NEGATION OF NEGATION / The law of the negation of negation is fundamental to dialectics. Every phenomenon, because internally contradictory, contains in itself its own proper negation (or its own opposite). Thus, within it unfolds the conflict between what *was* and what is *becoming* — between old and new. Negation of the past state is not, however, a pure or vain negation, a simple annulment of everything which has been (as metaphysics thinks.) "Negation, in dialectics, does not signify merely saying No, or simply saying something does not exist, or destroying it in some manner." (Engels) Dialectics demands "demonstration of the relation between the negative and the positive: so as to encounter the positive in the negative." (Lenin) Communism, thus, declares that everything positive has been created by humanity — even what was obtained under the yoke of capitalism. This is the positive in the negative. Communist society, in its turn, is the negation of the exploitative class regime — i.e. the negation of the negation.

OBJECTIVE / Opposite of subjective: what exists outside human consciousness, independently, but which human thought genuinely reflects.

PANTHEISM / (from the Greek, *pan*: all, and *theos*: god) Philosophical doctrine according to which divinity, as a spiritual and impersonal first principle, is found throughout nature — so that everything is divine.

PLATO / (427-347 B.C.) Greek philosopher, ideologist of the slave-owning aristocracy; founder of objective idealism which maintains that there exists besides the universe of perceptible things *another* world — the one of Ideas. So, above and beyond the trees one actually sees (which derive from various essences), Plato affirms there exists *the* unique Idea one has of 'trees', which is always identical, eternal — and this is the case for all of nature. According to Plato, things are only the shadows of Ideas. Ideas are eternal; things transitory. Not perception, but reason and its concepts give one true knowledge of the essence of things in reality.

PHILOSOPHY / (from the Greek, *philos*: love, friend, and *sophia*: science or wisdom) In dialectical materialism, the science of the most general laws of nature, human society and thought. The fundamental problem of philosophy is that of the relation between existence and thought. To find the answer, all philosophical tendencies divide up into two camps — materialist and idealist.

PHILOSOPHY, THE CLASSICAL GERMAN / Of the 18th and first half of the 19th centuries. Kant, its founder, was succeeded by Fichte and Schelling. Hegel's system represents the culminating phase of this philosophical movement. Classical German philosophy reflects the influences of European revolutionary movements. But such influences were deflected by the retrogressive socio-economic conditions of the epoch. This philosophy did contribute something fundamental — the renewal of dialectics as the theory of development. Taken up by Marx, it served as the basis for dialectical materialism. Engels has brilliantly analysed this philosophy in his work, "Ludwig Feuerbach And The End Of Classical German Philosophy."

POSITIVISM / One of the most widespread of the idealist currents within modern bourgeois philosophy. Positivism, according to its founders, is based not upon abstract deductions but on 'positive', real facts. August Comte, its creator, believed that the human mind must renounce any effort to know the very essence of things and content itself with the truth derived from observation and experiment. But this is only an "up to date" agnosticism.

PROPERTY / Private property appeared long after the origins of humanity. In the primitive communal state, ownership of the means of production was held in common. In the slave state, the 'boss' was the owner of human means of production — and hence the origin of private property. Under socialism, the means of production belong to the community, not to particular individuals — hence *socialist* property.

RATIONALISM / Theory which tends to recognize reason as the unique source of true knowledge; contrary to *empiricism* which makes perception this source of knowledge. Descartes and Leibnitz were outstanding representatives of rationalism.

RELATIONS OF PRODUCTION / Reciprocal relations established between people in the process of producing material goods. Persons can produce goods, not only individually, but together by uniting and practising communal action. History determines five main types of such relations: 1) In the primitive communal state, ownership of the instruments of production and products was held in common. With the passage from stone tools to metal, the tribes turned to agriculture and commerce and began to accumulate commodities. This led to the birth of private property, and monopolizing of accumulated wealth by a minority, and the rise of classes – the owners and the slaves. 2) In the slave epoch, free labour was replaced by slave exploitation: land was parcelled out to his serfs who worked for him partly freely, partly by payment in kind. 4) With the rise of the bourgeois or pre-capitalist society, a minority capitalist class seizes the means of production and exploits a wage-earning class. 5) The socialist state restores common ownership of the means of production, gives the product back to the producer, and eliminates ruling class exploitation.

RELIGION / Combination of beliefs and cult-practices which subordinates human life to a divine super-order. It appears in history as a form of oppression of the people by the ruling class. Marxism sees in religion the exploitation of human ignorance and credulity.

REVISIONISM / Hostile counter-current to Marxism which seeks to 'correct' he philosophical foundations of dialectical materialism. Today, for instance, China and the USSR accuse each other of 'revisionism' in their modes of applying socialism.

SCHOLASTICISM / (from Latin, *schola*, school; and Greek *skhole*, leisure) Gathered under this name are the various schools of philosophy current in the Middle Ages. But each one was linked strictly to religious dogma, all equally "servants of theology", all overlooked nature. Such dogmatism lends its name, 'scholastic', to all reasoning foreign to reality, all groundless philosophies, certain political discussions, etc. The main scholastics (or school-men) were Thomas Aquinas, Anselm of Canterbury, Duns Scotus, William of Occam, etc.

SOCIALISM / Economy, social and political doctrine which expresses the struggle for the equal distribution of wealth by eliminating private property and the exploitative ruling class. In practice, such a distribution of wealth is achieved by *social* ownership of the means of production, exchange and diffusion.

SOCIALISM (UTOPIAN) / Non-scientific socialism based on imaginary or optimist theories. Upheld by certain French and English utopian-socialists of the 19th century.

SOCIOLOGY / Science of society; as founded by Comte and Herbert Spencer, it takes no account of class struggle. Marx succeeded in raising sociology to a science by demonstrating that the development of society is not solely determined by *ideas* but by the *relations* of production. Thus he showed the course of ideas obeys the course of things. Marx also made clear that the problem of scientific research into society consists of the explanation of those particular historical laws which regulate the origin, existence, development and decline of any given social organism, and its transformation into another, superior one.

SOPHISM, SOPHISTRY / Incorrect reasoning presented in such a way as to appear correct, or persuasive, and thus which leads others into error. Sophistry is the application in discussion of such erroneous conclusions. The characteristic method of sophistry is: "To start from external resemblances between facts, apart from their relation to events." (Lenin) By relying on apparent resemblances, sophists seek to apply the properties of one set of phenomena to others completely different.

SPINOZA, BARUCH / (1632-77) Jewish-Dutch philosopher, denied the existence of God as creator of nature. Considered that God was nature itself. By thus calling nature God, he explained that nature was its own cause. He continued the rationalism of Descartes, although his system was monist – a system in which thought originates in nature.

STATE / Political organization of the economically dominant class, having as its aim the defence of the existing economic order (status quo) – but also the annihilation of the resistance put up against it by other classes. "The state is a machine to maintain the domination of one class over another." (Lenin)

TIME AND SPACE / These represent the objective form of the existence of matter. Time and space are inseparable from matter, and vice-versa. Dialectical materialism teaches that nothing exists in the world outside of or beyond matter in motion, and that matter cannot move except in space and time. Opposing itself to materialism, idealism believes time and space to be products of human thought and it separates these categories from matter.

THEOLOGY / Pseudo-science which seeks to give foundation to religion by borrowing from philosophical argumentation.

THESIS, ANTITHESIS, SYNTHESIS / (from the Greek: affirmation, negation, union) Every process of development, according to Hegel passes through these three stages: thesis, anti-thesis, syn-thesis. Each stage refutes the one before, and the last re-unites in itself the dominant features of the first two — hence its name, 'synthesis'. This is the 'surface' aspect of dialectics.

UNITY AND CONFLICT BETWEEN CONTRARIES / Opposing metaphysics, dialectics posits on principle that internal contradictions belong properly to all objects and natural phenomena, and within them everything is continually in motion, ever-changing. Each thing represents in itself the unity of contraries. Everything has a past and a future, a development and a decline, a positive and a negative aspect. This is why movement from a lower to a higher state is achieved by the struggle between opposite tendencies. Within the capitalist mode of production, the proletariat and the bourgeoisie are at once related and opposed through struggle.

...also from our catalogue

CUBA FOR BEGINNERS

by

HERE, IN COMIC BOOK FORM, FIDEL'S CIGAR SMOKING GUERILLAS TAKE ON UNCLE SAM AND HIS DIRTY TRICKS. BUT MORE – THIS IS A HISTORY OF CUBA IN CARTOONS, GOING RIGHT BACK TO COLUMBUS, THE SPANISH COLONIZATION, CUBA'S INDEPENDENCE STRUGGLES, ITS STATUS AS A QUASI-COLONY OF THE U.S., AND UP TO THE SOCIALIST REVOLUTION. A PAINLESS WAY TO LEARN SOME HISTORY! PLUS LOTS OF LAUGHTER...

85p.

ISBN 0904613 03 8

... in preparation – two more 'Beginners'

LENIN FOR BEGINNERS

CHRIST FOR BEGINNERS

BELIEVERS OR UNBELIEVERS – BEWARE! ...

RIUS ASKS CHALLENGING QUESTIONS WHICH MAY UPSET YOUR IDEAS! HE GOES BACK INTO HISTORY AND ASKS THE QUESTION OLDER THAN CHRISTIANITY ITSELF:

WAS CHRIST A MAN OF FLESH AND BLOOD – OR GOD?...

OR WAS HE MADE INTO A GOD?

The Dead Sea commune was full of subversives ... and Jesus was one of them ... in fact, a political leader...

...and still more!! new, original political

CAPITAL FOR BEGINNERS

by
PHIL EVANS

HEY! 'CAPITAL'? YOU DON'T MEAN DAS KAPITAL BY KARL MARX DO YOU?!? C'MON,— IN CARTOON FORM? Y'GOTTA BE KIDDING! WHY NOT EINSTEIN OR SOMETHING!

We understand your disbelief, but read what Phil Evans has to say...

comic books for 1977...

IRELAND FOR BEGINNERS